The Development of Western Civilization

*Narrative Essays in the History of Our Tradition from
Its Origins in Ancient Israel and Greece to the Present*

Edited by Edward W. Fox

*Professor of Modern European History
Cornell University*

THE ANCIENT GREEKS

By MORTON SMITH

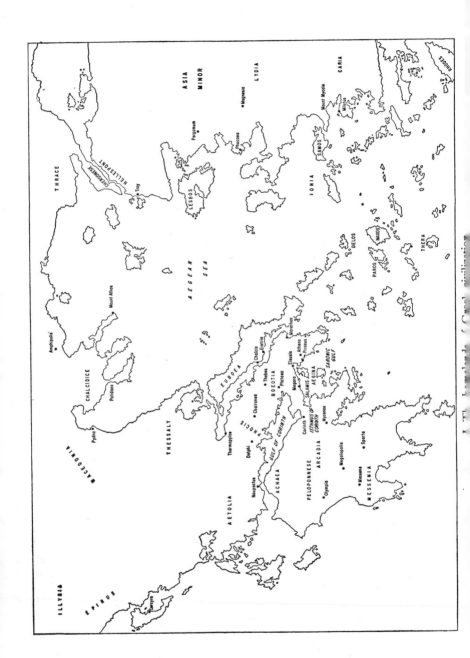

1. The homelands of Greek civilization

THE ANCIENT
GREEKS

MORTON SMITH, 1915—

COLUMBIA UNIVERSITY

Cornell University Press

ITHACA AND LONDON

© *1960 by Cornell University*

CORNELL UNIVERSITY PRESS

First published 1960
Second printing 1961
Third printing 1963
Fourth printing, with revisions, 1965
Fifth printing 1965
Sixth printing 1967
Seventh printing 1968
Eighth printing 1970

International Standard Book Number 0–8014–9852–x

PRINTED IN THE UNITED STATES OF AMERICA

BY THE VAIL-BALLOU PRESS, INC.

Foreword

THE proposition that each generation must rewrite history is more widely quoted than practiced. In the field of college texts on western civilization, the conventional accounts have been revised, and sources and supplementary materials have been developed; but it is too long a time since the basic narrative has been rewritten to meet the rapidly changing needs of new college generations. In the mid-twentieth century such an account must be brief, well written, and based on unquestioned scholarship and must assume almost no previous historical knowledge on the part of the reader. It must provide a coherent analysis of the development of western civilization and its basic values. It must, in short, constitute a systematic introduction to the collective memory of that tradition which we are being asked to defend. This series of narrative essays was undertaken in an effort to provide such a text for an introductory history survey course and is being published in the present form in the belief that the requirements of that one course reflected a need that is coming to be widely recognized.

Now that the classic languages, the Bible, the great historical novels, even most non-American history, have dropped out of the normal college preparatory program, it is imperative that a text in the history of European civilization be fully self-explanatory. This means not only that it must begin at the beginning, with the origins of our civilization in ancient Israel and Greece, but that it must introduce every name or event that takes an integral place in the account and ruthlessly delete all others no matter how firmly imbedded in historical protocol. Only thus simplified and complete will the narrative present a sufficiently clear outline of those major trends and developments that have led from the beginning of our recorded time to the most pressing of our current problems. This simplification, however, need not involve intellectual dilution or evasion. On the contrary, it can effectively raise rather than lower the level of presentation. It is on this assumption that the present series has been based, and each contributor has been urged to write for a mature and literate audience. It is hoped, therefore, that the essays may also prove profitable and rewarding to readers outside the college classroom.

The plan of the first part of the series is to sketch, in related essays, the narrative of our history from its origins to the eve of the French Revolution; each is being written by a recognized scholar and is designed to serve as the basic reading for one week in a semester course. The developments of the nineteenth and twentieth centuries will be covered in a succeeding series which will provide the same quantity of reading material for each week of the second semester. This scale of presentation has been adopted in the conviction that any understanding of the central problem of the preservation of the integrity and dignity of the individual human being depends first on an examination of the origins of our tradition in the politics and philosophy of the ancient Greeks and the religion of the ancient Hebrews and then on a relatively more detailed knowledge of its recent development within our industrial urban society.

The decision to devote equal space to twenty-five centuries and to a century and a half was based on the analogy with the human memory. Those events most remote tend to be remembered in least detail but often with a sense of clarity and perspective that is absent in more recent and more crowded recollections. If the roots of our tradition must be identified, their relation to the present must be carefully developed. The nearer the narrative approaches contemporary times, the more difficult and complicated this becomes. Recent experience must be worked over more carefully and in more detail if it is to contribute effectively to an understanding of the contemporary world.

It may be objected that the series attempts too much. The attempt is being made, however, on the assumption that any historical development should be susceptible of meaningful treatment on any scale and in the realization that a very large proportion of today's college students do not have more time to invest in this part of their education. The practical alternative appears to lie between some attempt to create a new brief account of the history of our tradition and the abandonment of any serious effort to communicate the essence of that tradition to all but a handful of our students. It is the conviction of everyone contributing to this series that the second alternative must not be accepted by default.

In a series covering such a vast sweep of time, few scholars would find themselves thoroughly at home in the fields covered by more than one or two of the essays. This means, in practice, that almost every essay should be written by a different author. In spite of apparent drawbacks, this procedure promises real advantages. Each contributor will be in a position to set higher standards of accuracy and insight in an essay encompassing a major portion of the field of his life's work than could ordinarily be expected in surveys of some ten or twenty centuries. The inevitable discontinuity of style and interpretation could be modified by editorial co-ordination; but it was felt that some discontinuity was in itself desirable. No illusion is more easily acquired by the student in an elementary course, or is more prejudicial to the efficacy of such a course, than that a single smoothly articulated text represents the very substance of history itself. If the shift from author to author, week by week, raises difficulties for the beginning student, they are difficulties that will not so much impede his progress as contribute to his growth.

This essay, *The Ancient Greeks*, by Mr. Morton Smith, is written to introduce the reader to the lively, restless, curious, and imaginative people who inhabited the Aegean world in the eleventh through third centuries B.C. Although the beginner in the field of European history is likely to know somewhat more about the civilization of the ancient Greeks than about that of most other early peoples, he is likely also to have glimpsed it through the golden haze of the traditional humanistic style of classical scholarship. Mr. Smith has achieved the unusual and refreshing feat of presenting the well-known heroes, writers, artists, statesmen, and philosophers in the cold light of everyday, where they can be seen at their intensely human—if still awe-inspiring —activities of fighting, farming, trading, arguing, playing, building: in short, creating that world of city-states which served as no other human institution to educate its members and posterity.

The author and the editor wish to express their gratitude for helpful suggestions to Mr. Arthur D. Nock, Mr. Moses Hadas, and Mr. Elias Bickerman.

EDWARD WHITING FOX

Ithaca, New York
June, 1960

Contents

Maps

THE ANCIENT GREEKS

By MORTON SMITH

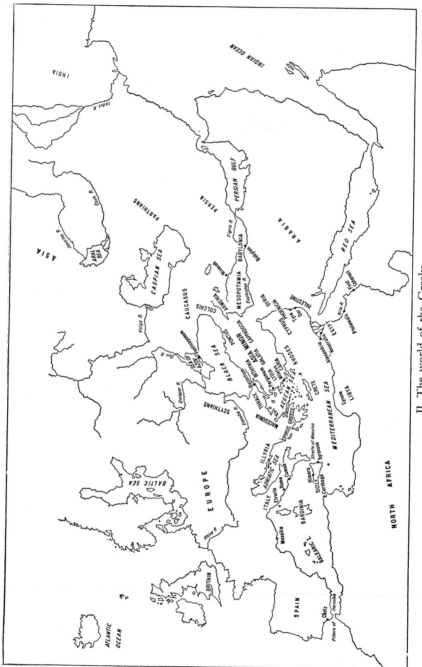

II. The world of the Greeks

CHAPTER I

Beginnings ~~~~~~~~~~~~~~~~~~~~~~~~~~~~~~~~

GREEK culture developed around the Aegean Sea. Such parts of the Greek mainland as were important in the process were almost all coastal areas and mostly on the east coast of the peninsula. With them, the islands of the Aegean and the west coast of Asia Minor early took a major part in shaping the new civilization. And it was across seas, from the islands and coastlands of the Aegean, that the culture spread, to the shores of the Black Sea and the coasts of Italy, Sicily, and North Africa. In the Greeks, then, we have a people situated not on a land mass, but around a sea, a people who think of earlier times as a series of "thalassocracies," of periods when one or another power controlled the seaways.

Across the southern end of the Aegean Sea lies the island of Crete. Here civilization had begun to rise above the neolithic level at about the end of the fourth millennium B.C., when the use of copper was introduced apparently from Syria or southern Asia Minor. Trade with Egypt and with the islands of the Aegean accelerated this development, and by the end of the third millennium the island saw the flowering of a brilliant culture. The ruins of great, unfortified palaces testify to the wealth of the rulers, the stability of the domestic government, and the control of the seas, which gave security from foreign enemies. The remains of towns from a somewhat later period testify to a considerable middle class, with a surprisingly high standard of living. Above all, a native artistic tradition, of unusual elegance and vitality, has left us frescoes, engraved gems, metal work, terra cottas, pottery, and carvings in stone and ivory. These show an amazing sense of color and feeling for line and an interest in movement which is unparalleled among the artistic works of the ancient Near East. They show a people, luxurious, sensuous, with both an intense delight in the human body and a liveliness in its representation, a people delighting in athletics, in boxing and displays of agility, but also in the world around them, in flowers and animals and the grotesque shapes of marine creatures. Among these remains are some which throw light on the religious practices current in the culture. Statuettes of goddesses or priestesses holding serpents have analogues in later Greek religion, and we can see, also, that bulls' horns and the double axe were important religious symbols. It is not unlikely that the powers of the underworld and of fertility were worshiped, particularly in the form of one or more great goddesses, but the subject remains speculative.

This Cretan culture has been called the Minoan, from a legendary king of Crete named Minos. Minoan culture was carried by traders to the shores of the countries around the eastern end of the Mediterranean. To Egypt and Syria, which had highly developed civilizations of their own, it contributed little. But in Greece about 1600 [1] it inspired a new culture, the Mycenaean, named from the town of

[1] All dates are B.C. unless otherwise specified.

Mycenae in the Peloponnese.[2] The remains of this culture are widely distributed and are especially frequent around the coasts of the Peloponnese and up the eastern coast of Greece as far as Thessaly. They are sprinkled also across the southern islands of the Aegean and along the west coast of Asia Minor and are frequent in Rhodes. From Rhodes the Mycenaeans evidently moved on about 1400 to colonize Cyprus. At the same time their trading settlements in some towns along the Syrian coast became so important that they must have been almost in control of the towns. They carried on an extensive trade with Egypt, and in the west their connections extended to south Italy and Sicily. Such an expansion of trade was possible only at the expense of their Minoan rivals. From about 1500 on there is evidence that the Mycenaeans were replacing the Minoans as carriers and were manufacturing cheap imitations of Minoan ware. In the years following 1400 many sites in Crete were sacked and burned. It is plausible to attribute the destruction to Mycenaean raiders. From this time on, Minoan culture rapidly declined.

Mycenaean culture differed from Minoan in a number of respects. Instead of the rambling Cretan palaces the Mycenaeans often built fortified citadels of which the interior plans were at least relatively simple and well organized: a central sequence of courtyards and vestibules leading to a great hall with a hearth in the center. The fortification shows a military concern which often appears in Mycenaean art and is absent from most Cretan work. Mycenaean art gen-

[2] The Peloponnese is often referred to by another transliteration as the Peloponnesus. Since Greek does not transliterate accurately into English, students must expect to find variations in the spelling of Greek geographical terms in common usage.

erally is cruder and more vigorous, less decorative and more narrative, less concerned with women and with religious subjects, more apt to show horses and hunting, than is Minoan art. Amber is more frequent in Mycenaean remains and argues closer trading connections with northern Europe. Probably in the interests of trade, but perhaps also for military purposes, considerable road building was done around Mycenae. Elsewhere we find the Mycenaeans reclaiming marshlands by large drainage projects. Such public works suppose a supply of labor, probably forced, and capable organization.

Our knowledge of Mycenaean culture from archaeological remains can be filled out cautiously from such cultural memories in the Homeric poems as that which must lie behind the account of two rustic heroes entering the palace of a king:

They marveled at the house of the King nurtured of Zeus. For a glory as of the sun or of the moon shone from the high-roofed house of renowned Menelaüs. But when they had seen it to their satisfaction with their own eyes, they went and were bathed in well-polished bathtubs. Then, after the maids had washed them and anointed them with oil and wrapped woolen garments about them, they sat down on chairs beside Menelaüs the son of Atreus [*Odyssey* 4. 43–51].[3]

And not only such general recollections of ancient glory, but even a number of details, references to the shapes of shields, for instance, have been proved by archaeological discoveries to be true to Mycenaean fashion.

These correspondences have been thought to prove the substantial truth of the historical events reported by the

[3] [The English translations of Greek texts cited in this essay are by the author. *Ed.*]

poetic tradition behind the Homeric poems: Paris, a prince of Troy, visited the court of Menelaüs, King of Sparta, and went off with Helen, Menelaüs' wife. Agamemnon, King of Mycenae, Menelaüs' brother, organized a Greek expedition to get her back. The Trojans refused to give her up and the Greeks therefore besieged Troy for ten years. The city was finally taken by a stratagem—the Greeks pretended to go away, but left a huge wooden horse filled with soldiers; the Trojans breached their walls to get the object inside their city; that night the soldiers emerged and their friends returned. After the destruction of the city the Greek warriors went back to their homes, encountering various adventures on their various ways. When excavation of Troy showed that a city there had, in fact, been destroyed toward the end of the thirteenth century, the main outlines of the story above were thought to have been confirmed. But the ruins of the city do not prove that it was sacked for the reasons or by the people reported, and the historical value of the Trojan story remains dubious.

Between the most plausible date for the Trojan war, the last half of the thirteenth century, and the most plausible date for the present form of the Homeric poems, the ninth or eighth century, lie the dark ages of Greek history. They began with a wave of invasion across Asia Minor and down the Syrian coast, destroying the ancient civilizations of those areas as well as the more recent Mycenaean markets there. The invaders were beaten off from Egypt shortly after 1200, but kept their hold on the Syrian coast. Their piratical activities must have cut into the trade between Egypt and Mycenae. It is probable that Greece was invaded at the same time. Mycenae was destroyed about 1150, but whether by invaders or domestic revolution is uncertain. The archaeological finds at excavated sites show no sudden introduction of a new culture, but rather a gradual deterioration of the traditional styles in the manufacture of pottery and other artifacts. It is likely, however, that a ruling class of invaders would have made the natives work for them, so the archaeological evidence does not prove that no invasion occurred. Greek traditions tell of several tribal movements in the three centuries after the Trojan war: a group of tribes called the Dorians moved from northern through central Greece into the Peloponnese, of which they occupied the southern and eastern regions up to and including the Isthmus of Corinth; hence they pushed on through Crete and the southernmost Aegean islands to Rhodes and the southwest corner of Asia Minor. The Achaeans, whom the Homeric poems show ruling in Mycenae and the southern Peloponnese, now moved to the northern coast of the Peloponnese and drove out the Greeks who had been living there, who belonged to a group called the Ionians. These Ionians with the help of kinsmen from the neighborhood of Athens, and of other groups also, took over the central islands of the Aegean and the central area of the west coast of Asia Minor, while a similar migration by another group, the Aeolians, occupied the island of Lesbos and the northern section of the coast up to the Hellespont.

Of all these movements the dates and details are uncertain and the uncertainty extends to the definition of the groups concerned and of the Greeks in general. If we define the Greeks as those who used the Greek language, then there must have been Greeks in both the Minoan and the Mycenaean civilizations, for in the remains of both have been found documents written in a syllabic script known as

"Linear B," and these are composed in an early form of Greek. Further, the Greek population of Cyprus was evidently planted there by Mycenaean invasion. On the other hand, several other sorts of writing were current in Minoan culture and were probably used to write other languages. A considerable non-Greek population survived on Crete, Cyprus, and several islands of the Aegean and in some places of mainland Greece down to historical times. And Greek tradition reported that large non-Greek elements went into the make-up of the Ionians, in particular.

What is certain from the remains is that much of the Mycenaean cultural tradition was gradually lost. Monumental building disappeared. The spirals and curved lines of Mycenaean decoration gradually hardened into the circles and zigzags and "Greek keys" of a style known appropriately as the geometric. In pottery, the appearance of a great variety of wares, none of which is distributed over any considerable area, testifies to the decline of trade. The average level of technical skill shown in figurines and utensils sank to the level of barbarism. Writing disappeared.

Gradually a new cultural tradition began to establish itself, not only on the Greek mainland, but also in Ionia— that part of the coast of Asia Minor and its offshore islands settled by the Ionians. Mycenaean settlements had been planted here in the period before the invasions. Many later settlers may have come as refugees from the invaders of the mainland and have brought with them elements of the older civilization. We have seen that such elements are preserved in the Homeric poems, and the Homeric poems are the products of this new development. They stand at the beginning of Greek literature, at once the summary and supreme achievement of its peculiar virtues. Concerned with man rather than the gods or the physical world, with individuals rather than society, but above all with men in their relations to each other, they have an intense delight in the strength and beauty of their bodies, the dexterity of actions, the power of speech and the glory of song, a dramatic delight which is the more intense because they see the human drama as a tragedy: Men are not like the blessed gods who live forever; the hero must kill and be killed; the traveler's destination is the grave. From the time of these poems forever the Greeks were set apart from all other peoples of the ancient world by the importance to them of the poetry of men.

The traditions about Homer, his blindness and his wanderings, may or may not have some historical basis, but the skillful construction of the *Iliad* and the *Odyssey* makes it probable that each was edited, if not composed, by a single genius. This is argued, too, by the peculiar position of the poems in Greek literature. They are far from containing all the material dealing with the Trojan cycle. The *Iliad* treats only of one incident toward the end of the war: Achilles, the best fighter on the Greek side, was insulted by Agamemnon and withdrew from the fighting. After his friend Patroclus was killed by the Trojan hero, Hector, he returned and killed Hector. The *Odyssey* treats only of the adventures of one hero, Odysseus, his wanderings after the siege of Troy and his return to kill the suitors who had moved into his household on the pretext of courting his wife, Penelope, and were plotting to murder his son, Telemachus. There was a large body of traditional poetry dealing with the other episodes of the war and its aftermath. Some of this poetry was cast into epic form by other poets, and some of their poems were occasionally attributed, by individual critics, to Homer; but throughout antiquity the *Iliad* and the *Odyssey* held a place apart. On the other hand, it is doubtful that the same man produced both, and it is certain that both contain, not only general cultural tradition, but also accumulations of poetic material from the dark ages whence they both emerge. Both represent poets as singers attached to royal courts, who sang for the pleasure of their patrons, especially during and after meals, and who celebrated in their songs the deeds of famous men. Both present a common picture of the rulers for whom the court poets of the dark ages sang, and of their society, as those rulers wished to see it.

The king was primarily the leader of his people in war. When they were not at war he lived, in his great house, the life of a country gentleman, concerning himself with management of his estate, sacrifice to the gods, and maintenance of order among his people. Of his domestic virtues the poets most emphasized hospitality to strangers (a virtue in which they themselves had an interest). The essential royal virtues, however, were those of the military leader— wisdom in planning, courage, skill in fighting, physical strength. Leadership had first to be exercised in the small circle of the king's council, the chiefs of the families or tribes over which he ruled. Here, too, he needed the other virtues characteristic of a warlike society, especially an extreme courtesy in dealing with men who were intensely concerned about their personal honor and apt to fight. The same courtesy was shown in dealing with women, especially of the upper class, and was normally extended to persons of lower class, so long as they knew their place and behaved accordingly.

Next in rank beneath the chiefs came their free male

followers, and these, both in peace and in war, formed an assembly which had to be won over to carry out the leader's proposals. That a member of the assembly, even in wartime, should speak against the leader was not unknown; when the situation arose, the leader might deal with it by giving the offender a public beating and threatening to strip him naked if he repeated the offense. This treatment would be most effective if the offender were ugly or, better yet, a cripple—to these poets a cripple was always good for a laugh. Such measures, however, were not usually necessary, particularly if the leader had that form of wisdom which was most admired—skill in speaking. To speak well in the assembly or the council was a gift of the gods, and the assembly in particular was, like the battle, the place where men attained honor. Since the Homeric poems soon became and long remained the standard texts memorized in elementary education, they exerted an immense influence throughout antiquity and in modern times by presenting this ideal of the gentleman.

For a people living on the shores of a sea, warfare, piracy, and trade were at first hardly distinguishable. So the king was also the leader in maritime adventures, in which the methods were adapted to the opportunities. Travel by sea was dangerous. The waters were uncharted and the ships were tiny—down to the beginning of the fifth century even warships customarily had no more than fifty oars. With oars and with a single removable mast on which a single square sail could be hoisted, they crept along from headland to headland, island to island, avoiding whenever possible the open sea. At night the ships were beached and the men camped on the shore. Yet by these methods they had already in Homeric times made the circuit of the

Mediterranean and gone beyond it. The stories of Odysseus' adventures reflect not only the legends of the ancient Near East, but also the yarns of sailors who had already been wind-bound on sand bars off Egypt, escaped from savages in Sicily, scraped through the straits of Messina, conversed with nymphs on the islands of the western Mediterranean, and sailed across the Black Sea to the magic land of Colchis and the misty marshes of the great rivers of the North, the land of the dead.

This world was full of gods. Almost any fortunate or unfortunate or extraordinary or important occurrence— the impulse to shoot an arrow, the fact that it hit or missed its target, the sort of wound it made if it did hit—was apt to be attributed to "a god" or "the god," without further identification. Besides this naïve piety, however, the Homeric poems describe a society of particular gods with local habitations, names, and well-defined characteristics. They are represented, roughly speaking, as members of the Homeric aristocracy, but with supernatural powers and subnormal inhibitions. As such they were conveniences for lively narrative and for the expression of ideas which in later literature were represented by the use of abstract terms. In concrete Homeric Greek it is impossible to say, abstractly, that the supernatural power which sanctions marriage worked to bring about the downfall of Troy. And even if possible, the abstract statement would have been colorless, an objection which cannot be brought against the Homeric way of putting things: Hera so hated the Trojans that she wanted to walk through the gates and eat them raw. Just how far Homer or the poets before him deliberately or unconsciously, in the process of literary creation, developed this naturalistic picture of the gods, we can never be sure. On the one hand, some Greeks early came to believe that the picture was largely due to the influence of the Homeric poems. On the other, there is no doubt that the poems built on popular concepts and cults of the gods who figured largest in them: Zeus, god of the sky, Poseidon of the sea and of earthquakes, Hera of marriage, Athena of wisdom and skills (including warfare), Aphrodite of sexual pleasure, Apollo of the arts of young men (especially archery, music, and prophecy), Artemis of wild things (hence childbirth and hunting), Hephaestus of fire and metallurgy, Hermes of roads, and Ares of the fury of battle. From the earliest times, therefore, Greek religion contained the antithesis (which was to be important for philosophy) between general piety toward an indefinite divine power and specific worship of particular gods about whom fairly definite conceptions were current. By creating extremely anthropomorphic pictures of the gods and by giving these pictures the widest circulation, the Homeric poems sharpened the antithesis, but they did not create it.

Moreover, important as kingship and war and seafaring and the Homeric gods might be, they were all secondary to the essential concern of the great majority of the Greeks of the dark ages. That concern was getting food out of the ground. Ancient Greece, including Ionia and the islands, was always a largely agricultural society, and in early days, at least, the agricultural concern was far more important than any other.

The poet in whose work the agricultural side of life first found full expression, Hesiod, lived probably at the end of the eighth century, within a hundred years or less of the completion of the Homeric poems. Like the Homeric authors, he had connections with Asia Minor—his father had come from there to mainland Greece—and he used the meter and much of the vocabulary of the Homeric poems. But where the poets of the courtly tradition are known merely by inference, Hesiod thrusts himself on our attention as an individual of a lower class who wants his rights and is determined to be heard. He did not compose for the amusement of a court circle, but for practical purposes: to ridicule a shyster brother who was trying to do him out of his share of the family estate, to counterbalance his brother's bribes and set him an example of a way of life by which to earn an honest living.

The way of life Hesiod described in his poem entitled *Works and Days* was that which occupied most of the time of most of the Greeks from the tenth to the fifth centuries: ploughing in November and December, surviving the cold in January, pruning vines in February and March, sailing in April and May, reaping in May and June, threshing and winnowing in July, sailing again in July and August, vintage in September, woodcutting in October.[4] Along with agriculture, sailing was conspicuous, although Hesiod himself did not like it. The small farmer might also dabble in trade (or piracy). This versatility was a consequence both of the geographical position of the Greeks as a people around a sea and of the long, dry Mediterranean summer, with its months of enforced agricultural idleness in fine weather—a season made for sailing, fishing, fighting, athletic

---

[4] Notice that this is a man's calendar. It says almost nothing of the important domestic industries which were the work of women —the preparation of food and the manufacture of textiles. Also it says almost nothing of pottery and of metal work, which were done by men but were already, to a large extent, in the hands of relatively few specialists.

competitions, the recitation of epic poetry, and interminable conversations on every subject under the sun. Most of the rest of the year was filled with the drudgery of farming. The two staple crops were grain, usually barley, and grapes. Grain was the gift of Demeter and wine of Dionysus, the two great gods of the peasants, neglected in the Homeric poems. Both had been worshiped in Mycenaean times, and the fact that their cults had survived the dark ages argues that the peasant population had not been generally uprooted by the invasions. Hesiod did not mention the olive, but it was already being grown for food and was to become the third staple of Greek agriculture, not only a food itself, but a source of oil for lighting, for cooking, and for anointing the body. Apart from the staples, the Greek farmer might have some fruit trees (apples, pears, and figs) and garden vegetables (onions were already an important element in the Greek atmosphere), beehives (honey served for sugar), sheep and goats for wool and milk, pigs, pigeons, geese, and, most important and expensive of all, oxen for ploughing. Horses and hunting dogs were for the nobles. Chickens were probably not introduced till the sixth or fifth century. Meat was a luxury for the peasant, to be had only on festivals when an animal was sacrificed. (The inedible parts were usually offered to the god, the edible, reserved for the worshipers.) In these circumstances, fish, which the Homeric heroes would eat only to save themselves from starving and which Hesiod scarcely mentions, became more popular; by the fifth century it was one of the major items of Greek diet.

CHAPTER II

The Brave New World

BARBARIAN invasions destroyed cities, but also created them. When the countryside was overrun by invaders, the natives took shelter in fortified centers. When the invaders settled down to internecine warfare, they in turn found such centers necessary to protect themselves from each other. Accordingly it is not surprising to find mention of fortified cities in the Homeric poems. Some of these cities, like Troy, may have been recollections of the Mycenaean age, but others undoubtedly belonged to later times. The city's primary defensive function was usually indicated not only by its walls, but also by its location on top of a hill or at the foot of some spur of rock, an "acropolis" to which the citizens could flee. By Hesiod's time, however, from a defensible refuge, the city had become also a center of trade and adjudication. Hesiod, though a farmer, was not a rustic; he and his brother had been at law before the judges of their city.

Ancient cities differed from modern ones most conspicuously in size. The Troy which Homer's heroes are supposed to have besieged for ten years covered about four acres, an area roughly four hundred feet on a side. About Hesiod's time Nineveh, the capital of the huge Assyrian empire, was famous for its vast extent. It was some three miles long by a mile wide. If you started from the center and walked in any direction you could reach the city wall in about twenty minutes at most. Outside the wall, you were in the country. Some outbuildings might cluster round and occasionally grow to be small suburbs, but there was nothing like the interminable suburban area which surrounds a modern city. Usually the wall was a sharp boundary, almost as important for its psychological as for its military consequences. Inside was home, outside were the bare fields and the sea, wild animals and strange men, the graveyards and the dead and supernatural beings.

The small size of the ancient city made its people aware of their dependence on the surrounding country and its life. Many of them were farmers who walked out, often for miles, to their fields. In harvest or vintage season, when the weather was fine and labor was needed, the whole family might go out and camp in the fields till the work was done. The difficulties of transporting food in bulk and the poverty of means for preserving it made the produce of the countryside a matter of literally vital concern to the city. Available foods changed greatly from one part of the year to another. The failure of any crop meant hardship, that of a major crop, famine. The festivals and fasts of the city, therefore, the basis of its religious and civic calendar, were principally those of the agricultural year: fertility rites in the fall and winter, when the grain was planted and the vines were pruned, rites of purification and protection while the crops were growing, and celebrations at harvest time in the early summer, at vintage time in the autumn, and at the times when the first loaves of the new grain were baked, the first fruits offered, and the new wine ready for drinking.

Within the city (unless there had recently been a pestilence, as was frequently the case) life was crowded. Behind the fortifications the houses of men and gods were huddled together in confusion. The palaces of Mycenaean times had disappeared, and one- or two-room huts, square, oval, or with one square and one rounded end, served for gods and men alike down to the seventh century.

In Minoan and Mycenaean times the gods had been worshiped either in special rooms of the palaces or in natural sanctuaries, notably caves. The tradition of worship without a temple never died out: to the end of classical times a sanctuary might be no more than an enclosed area. But sometime after the invasions houses began to be built for some gods, especially in the Aegean islands where the example of Near Eastern temples may have been at work. Here large Greek temples appeared as early as the eighth century. When it became customary, perhaps also as a result of Near Eastern influence, to represent the god by a large statue, the statue was usually placed inside the temple, against the middle of the back wall, facing out. But the Greeks never generally adopted the ritual by which many Near Eastern statues were daily wakened, dressed, fed, and entertained. Sacrifices were often thought of as food for the god, but were commonly offered by burning on an altar outside. Religious assemblies were normally outside, too. So the building merely housed the statue and some utensils. It had no need of complexity. It remained, essentially, the one-room hut. At most another room or a porch, or both, might be put on the front, or on the back, and the whole surrounded by a colonnade. Such is the floor plan even of the Parthenon, the great, fifth-century temple of Athena in Athens, the masterpiece of the Greek genius for magnificent yet simple development of a primitive theme.

Men's needs were more complex, so we find the plans of their houses developing. Sequences of three rooms, side by side or end to end, appeared in the seventh century. In the sixth century a plan utilizing an interior courtyard was adopted, probably from the Near East. It remained the standard to the end of the classical period. The house was built to the edge of the street; there was no surrounding yard. From the street one entered a passageway or outer room. Beyond this was a courtyard, off which opened the inner rooms. Most of the living went on in the courtyard. There might be a second story and, in big houses, several courtyards. In the sixth century, also, the roofs became flat (another example of Near Eastern influence?) and henceforth were used for drying food and clothes, cooking, eating, sleeping, and communications of all sorts—most houses adjoined their neighbors by party walls.

Between the houses, the streets were unpaved, crooked, and narrow (often only about ten feet wide). There was at least one open area, however, the market place or agora. Here went on not only business affairs, but gossip and official announcements, conversations, discussions, quarrels, the political and much of the social life of the city. Here too might be situated temples of popular resort. The chief temple would usually be on the acropolis, which would also be specially fortified and might be the site of other public buildings. But the nature of an acropolis was to be high and hard to climb, so buildings of everyday resort were usually located in more easily accessible areas. The agora was normally the most accessible place in the city.

The agora therefore witnessed the political development of the Greeks. That development began with loss of power by the kings to the heads of the great families, who made up their councils. This took place generally in the eighth and seventh centuries. The extent of the loss differed from place to place, but its effect was uniform: government by a single man gave way to government by the members of a small group. As the king was divested of his powers, competition for these between members of the group was probably often settled by the consideration of popular support, which came to mean by election, although candidates could be drawn only from the leading families. Election encourages hopes that the elected officials will not abuse their powers and that the privilege of rule, over a period of years, will be shared among the competitors. These hopes are more apt to be justified if offices are tenable for limited periods only. Limitation of tenure seems to have been made the rule in Athens by the end of the eighth century. By such steps the governing cliques of nobles— the "oligarchies"—in the various cities unwittingly created what were in effect constitutional laws. These "laws" first existed as practices or as understandings between the members of the ruling families. But once they had become fixed they could be appealed to, against any who neglected them, or attacked by any who wished a change. They came to be thought of as determining the form of the government. This conception of the state as shaped and governed by a body of laws which were independent of the will of the temporary ruler, but were not the utterances of some divinity, and therefore were capable of change by the people as a whole, was extremely rare in the civilizations of the ancient Near East, but was important in Greek history from the end of the eighth century on and in the subsequent history of the western world.

Along with this internal political development of the cities went an external one. Some cities gained control of areas as much as twenty or thirty miles long. Already in the beginning of the dark ages the legendary king Theseus of Athens had united all Attica under his rule. Attica is an inverted triangle about twenty miles across the base, and thirty-five from base to tip (as the crow flies). Theseus reportedly made all its people citizens of Athens and established a common council drawn from the ruling families of the whole territory. Thus a "city-state" might differ considerably from a city and include a number of minor towns. Such city-states, rarely with so much territory, grew up around the east coast of Greece from the Peloponnese as far north as Thessaly, all over the Aegean islands, and along the western coast of Asia Minor. Only in the district at the heart of the Peloponnese—a district of which the name "Arcadia" has become proverbial for "unspoiled country"—and in the central mountains of northern Greece and, to an extent, in Thessaly, was the development of city-states delayed till the fourth century and later.

The development of city-states was both aided and limited by the geographical characteristics of Greece, the Aegean Islands, and the coast of Asia Minor, a world of small but steep mountains and tiny river valleys, with almost no large plains. The cities found their expansion limited by natural boundaries. Therefore, since they had to expand, they turned to trade and then to colonization, financing expeditions by their citizens to seize land in the countries with which trade had acquainted them.

The occasional adventurers of Homer and the summer-time sailors of Hesiod were now followed by men for whom sea travel and the exchange of merchandise were regular and major, albeit seasonal, concerns. This development was the more rapid because the areas settled by the Greeks were poor in copper (except for Cyprus) and poorer in iron. Iron came largely from the highlands of eastern Asia Minor, and two arms of Greek trade went out to meet it along the northern and southern coasts of that great peninsula. On the other side of continental Greece, merchants early established trading connections across the Adriatic with southern Italy and with Etruria, where there were also important deposits of iron. This development of Greek trade drove foreigners—notably the Phoenicians—out of the Greek markets for a while, but brought the Greeks themselves directly into contact with foreign cultures.

The Phoenician traders thus driven out retained their own trading network from their own coast across the southern Mediterranean to the northwestern corner of Sicily and the opposite promontory of Africa, thence on to Sardinia, the Balearic Islands, and the coasts of Spain. From Spain they passed beyond the pillars of Hercules into the north Atlantic, where they established at Cádiz, on the Spanish coast, an important base for their trade with Britain. In Greece itself, traces of their influence survived in a number of religious traditions, in some elements of art and, perhaps, architecture, and in the use of the Phoenician alphabet as the basis of the Greek alphabet and number system (for the letters served as numbers, too). Other Near Eastern elements in Greek culture were survivals from far earlier times, and more were now introduced as a result of

Greek contact with Egypt, the Phoenician coast, and the interior of Asia Minor.

From Asia Minor came, with other things, the art of coinage, that is, of dividing precious metals into small pieces of standard quality, the quality being guaranteed by a stamp of some individual or institution on each piece. The plentiful existence of such guaranteed pieces facilitated business. Therefore the invention (which seems to have been put to official use first in Lydia in the neighborhood of 700) was adopted during the seventh century by the Greek trading cities along the coast of Asia Minor and quickly spread across the Aegean islands to the trading cities around the Isthmus of Corinth.

The growth of trade brought with it the development of technical skills, and trade and skills together laid open to the Greeks a new and wonderful world, theirs for the taking. The western reaches of the Mediterranean and the coasts of the Black Sea were only scantily inhabited, and the inhabitants were at a level of civilization much lower than that which the Greeks had now achieved. Therefore during the two centuries from 750 to 550 the Greeks were able to follow up their exploratory trading by the establishment of colonies. In this process the trading cities played the leading roles. Of those on the Ionian coast of Asia Minor, Miletus in the eighth century explored the Black Sea, and in the seventh ringed it with colonies; Phocaea, about 600, founded Massilia (modern Marseilles) whence a string of settlements stretched along the coasts of France and Spain. The Ionian cities of Chalcis and Eretria on the island of Euboea were also great colonizers: In the west Chalcis planted the earliest Greek colony on Italy at Cumae about 750 and followed this by a cluster of settlements on the northeast tip of Sicily and the toe of Italy; in the east its numerous colonies on Chalcidice gave that peninsula its name. Of the cities on the Isthmus and Gulf of Corinth, Corinth itself founded colonies along the savage west coast of northern Greece, and in Sicily it planted the greatest of all Greek colonies, Syracuse (734), but it established colonies also around the Aegean. Megara, at the other end of the Isthmus, founded a colony on Sicily and a cluster of settlements near the southwestern end of the Black Sea, the most famous of them being Byzantium (667). The cities along the Gulf of Corinth colonized the instep and toe of Italy so thoroughly that the area became known, with Sicily, as Greater Greece. Finally Rhodes was prominent in the colonization of the southern coast of Sicily, and the little island of Thera founded the great colony of Cyrene in Libya (630), chief of a cluster of Dorian colonies there.

All these colonies were in territories where there was no native power of sufficient size to resist the Greeks; Greek trading settlements in the Near East were on a different footing, but were part of the same general expansion. Most important of them was Naucratis in Egypt, founded in the latter half of the seventh century, the chief (and at times the only) trading port of the Greeks in that country. Miletus and the island cities of Samos and Aegina had concessions here, as did a union of the lesser cities of the Asia Minor coast and coastal islands.

This network of trading ports and colonies had a profound effect on the life of the Greek cities. The colonies served as bases for the expansion of the trading network, as sources of supply for raw materials and as markets for manufactured goods. Since Homeric times there had been steady progress in shipbuilding, and by the sixth century merchantmen frequently carried more than a hundred tons (although they still relied for propulsion on their one, oblong, central sail). With ships of this size, bulk trade became important. The pottery of Corinth, the metalware of Chalcis and Samos, the textiles of Samos and Miletus, and the wine and oil of mainland Greece were paid for by tin from Britain and lead from Spain (shipped through Massilia), hides and grain from Sicily and southern Italy, gold and silver, timber and tar from Macedonia and Thrace, salted fish, grain and slaves from the Black Sea region, amber from the Baltic (carried across Europe to the Black Sea ports), linen and glass from Phoenicia and Egypt, papyrus and ivory from Egypt, drugs and grain from Egypt and Libya. Fostered by this traffic, many colonies became rich. Almost all were independent of their mother cities, though usually bound to them by ties of religion and sentiment. (Corinth was an exception in trying to control its colonies, and its effort led to serious difficulties.) Facing new circumstances and free to adjust to them, the colonies during the first two centuries of their history were the frontier of the Greek world. They prevented its stagnation, extended its knowledge, criticized, modified, and neglected its customs, developed its ideas to conclusions sometimes exorbitant, gave it practice in city planning both physical and legal, provided it with examples of all sorts of social experiments and their consequences, sent back to it treasures and flamboyant millionaires, patronized its artists and philosophers, and were an area of exile for its obstreperous individuals. Most important of all, they absorbed the increase of its population and themselves increased its business. Thanks to them, the Aegean area was the center of a vast, expanding economy.

This economic expansion was reflected in the development of a brilliant oligarchic culture radically different from any the world had seen. The great families both ruled the older cities and provided the leaders of the colonial expeditions. They became wealthy and used their wealth to live luxuriously. This put their wealth back into circulation, and so continued the economic expansion. There was no great overlord, as there had been in the Near Eastern empires, to keep the local ruling class down by taxation or military pressure. Nor was the economic and intellectual environment dominated by the numerous clergy and vast endowments of great temples. The temple buildings remained of the simple sort described above. Often they had no hereditary priesthood and were served by individuals elected annually. Even when a priesthood was hereditary in some family, it was often no more than an avocation for the man who held it, requiring full-time attention only on a few annual festivals. Of course, there were exceptions. In Corinth hundreds, if not thousands, of sacred prostitutes were in the service of Aphrodite. In Delphi the oligarchy which controlled the famous oracle exercised much influence by interpreting its answers to questions on political affairs and by controlling its vast treasure; they constituted what might be called an important clerical interest in Greek politics. But these were outstanding exceptions. By and large, the Greek society which then appeared was characteristically secular. Its ruling class lived for honor and pleasure, love and adventure; wealth and political power were generally pursued as means to these.

Concern for honor and pleasure appeared in the creation of a multitude of great festivals. Greatest of all were the Olympic games, held every fourth year at Olympia in the western part of the Peloponnese. Here, protected by an international truce, came competitors from all parts of the Greek world, followed by throngs of observers, merchants, entertainers, servants, and miscellaneous hangers-on. Beside the contests (chariot and horse races, foot races, jumping, throwing the quoit and the javelin, wrestling, and boxing) and the attendant processions, sacrifices, and banquets, the games served as national fairs, where merchants, mountebanks and musicians displayed their wares, and all the world came to see and be seen. For persons living in small cities, with little privacy, personal prestige was of great importance. This was the great prize at the games. Nominally, the victor received only a wreath of wild olive, but he would be considered a public benefactor by his city, his return would be a triumph, and he would be given substantial rewards in money or privileges. So popular were the Olympic games that others were developed along the same lines, the most famous being the Pythian games at Delphi and the Isthmian and Nemean games near the Isthmus of Corinth. Also religious festivals in various cities were elaborated along the lines of the games (which themselves were nominally religious festivals) and became great public shows with contests in athletics and music and poetry as well as magnificent processions, choral songs, dances, and public feasts to supplement the sacrifices. Most famous of these were the Panathenaic festivals at Athens.

The popularity of athletic contests, and the concern for the human body which went with them, were traits already mentioned as characteristic of Minoan-Mycenaean culture.

Now they became of the greatest importance for the structure of Greek society and education.

"Society," in this world, was the society of men. Women of good family were married off young and were expected to remain in the women's quarters of their homes. They were prohibited from attending the games and many other spectacles. Marriage was a matter of arrangements, largely financial, with the father of the bride. It was thought of in terms of domestic economy and children. Children, in particular, were financial burdens; therefore—since methods of birth control were still primitive—a man often postponed marriage till his thirties and meanwhile found his sexual gratification either with slaves and prostitutes or in love. Love was conceived as, properly, a relationship between a man and an adolescent boy. In many cities it was expected that a boy between fourteen and nineteen would have a lover; the relationship was not only open and approved, but was thought an essential part of education for a boy of the upper class. The man was to initiate the boy into the customs of the world of men and to provide him an example of manliness. The center from which these love affairs began was the gymnasium, the place where men went naked (*gymnoi*), the club frequented by the men and boys of good family. This became the starting point of higher institutional education—primarily in music and physical training—and the center for discussions of politics, literature, and eventually philosophy.

The peculiar sensibility developed by this society was brilliantly reflected in its art and literature.

As for art, it may (or may not) be fanciful to think the concerns of a predominantly male society are expressed by the naked lines and solidity of the Doric temples built in this period, where decoration is peripheral and the beauty of the building is a function of its geometry. But there is no question that the sculpture of the seventh and sixth centuries expresses a new feeling for the male body, a new interest in its bareness, a new tactual concern for its plastic values, especially the modeling of its muscles.

At the same time, the art of these centuries shows the influence of Near Eastern trade. Especially in the trading city of Corinth there appeared a new style of pottery which luxuriated in oriental motifs—lotus flowers, palmettes, rosettes, fantastic animals, and mythological figures. The sculpture of the Ionian coast, where homosexuality was never so prominent as in the Dorian states, shows a delight in making elaborate patterns with ornaments and folds of drapery, especially of female figures, an interest in surface decoration which derives from Near Eastern art. Even in the Dorian style the basic figure of the standing male may have been derived from Egypt; its similarity to Egyptian figures makes clearer the difference of the Greek treatment, which reflects the difference of the Greek feeling for the male body.

Akin to this feeling is a more general delight in the actualities of the physical world, the variety of its shapes and textures and all the minutiae of daily life. Because of this delight, Greek work shows an increasing accuracy of observation and faithfulness of representation which culminated in a new artistic tradition radically different from that of the ancient Near East and destined to shape the aesthetic standards of the western world. The oriental motifs remained as marginal decorations, often to accentuate the simplicity of the central figures; the Near Eastern tradition of stylization continued to shape minor details—

the treatment of drapery and hair, for instance. But the major element was the new concern for the human figure and the world around it.

This concern appears with particular clarity on the Attic black-figure pottery of the late seventh and the sixth centuries. Its world is the world of the Greek aristocrat. Farming and manual labor of all sorts, the concerns of the lower classes, are rarely represented, but the picture of upper class life is almost complete. The gymnasium and the battle, the banquet and the funeral pyre, sacrifice and rape, checkers and suicide, Greeks and barbarians, deities and pet animals, women and mythological monsters—the whole world of upper-class imagination and activity bursts into life on this pottery, asserting itself in defiance of the natural limitations of painting on curved surfaces. As decoration this art is often unsuccessful. The figures are distorted by the shapes of the objects on which they are painted; the lines of the objects are broken by the horizontal stripes of the painting. The Chinese and the Egyptians had more respect for the pure beauty of the forms of utensils. The Greeks sacrificed aesthetics to their delight in representation of their multiform world.

The same delight, range of interest, and novelty of form appear in the Greek literature of the period, which shows an equally radical departure from that of the ancient Near East. The older forms continued to be produced; several second-rate epics appeared and the ancient "wisdom literature"—strings of allegedly wise sayings—was continued. (But characteristically, the most eminent writer in the form —Theognis, about 550—made it the vehicle less for traditional wisdom than for the expression of his own personality.) These older forms, though, were overshadowed by the development of a new Greek literature reflecting the new age: choral poetry for the festivals and for celebration of victors in the games, drinking songs for the banquets, satires and epigrams attacking political opponents, patriotic and military poems. Many of these forms had sources age old in popular song, but it is characteristic of this period that they now first appear as works of art for an upper class who want more than the old, popular songs and who will remember the new, literary forms as creations of particular individuals—creations which were to shape much of the poetry of the ancient and of the modern world.

Along with the new forms went a new use of poetry for personal expression, and expression of a new sort of personality. In this growing world of Greek commerce and colonization, where old ways were being questioned and new ones introduced, the expanding economy made it possible for men to break away from the ties of family and city and live as isolated individuals. At the same time the growing wealth of the upper class and the lack of restraint on it encouraged the growth of individualism among its members. This is not to say that individualism now appeared for the first time. We saw it already in Hesiod. But Hesiod accepted the standards of his society and based his claims on them. Archilochus of Paros, in the following century, was the product of the new world, the man who lives for himself, who is in the society, but not of it, thumbs his nose at its standards, and is bitter about his loneliness. Because of this loneliness the concerns of his personal life acquire for him an absolute importance which is the essence of much personal poetry from that time to this. Deepest of these concerns is love, and the greatest literary achievement of this age was its love poetry. No earlier civilization has left us any such poetry, and of much produced by later civilizations, little can compare with this. Supreme among the poets was Sappho of Lesbos, remembered not only for her celebration of that love between women which was the obverse of the homosexual love sung by many of these poets, but also for the passionate directness and power of her poems.

The ultimate achievement of individualism is to think for oneself. Therefore it is not surprising that in the trading cities of the Ionian coast, where the literature of individualism flourished, there appears also the beginning of systematic, rational speculation, that attempt to understand the nature of things which is basic both to science and to philosophy. The more ancient cultures had developed practical skills which testified to considerable reasoning, but when they had speculated about the nature of things they had done so in mythological terms, which do not enable those who use them to develop their thought by rational inference or criticism. The new achievement of the Greek philosophers was to apply to speculation about nature in general the rational method of observation and inference, and so to take the first step toward the reduction of human knowledge from a chaos of unrelated subjects to a single coherent system.

The beginning of this process is generally thought to have been made by Thales of Miletus. Thales was later believed to have had considerable knowledge of mathematics and astronomy and to have predicted the eclipse of 585 B.C. Whatever knowledge of these subjects he did have, he probably got from Near Eastern sources, most likely by way of Egypt, where Miletus had trading connections. Perhaps from the same sources he had the notion that water was first of all things and that all things somehow came from it. The question was how they came. The Babylonians had said the primeval waters were a monster killed by a god who split her like a shellfish and made the sky of one half and the ocean of the other; this is pure mythology, description of physical processes in terms proper to animal life. The Egyptians had said the earth emerged from the primal waters as a hillock emerges from a receding flood; this is legend which provides no explanation of the event it reports. What Thales said we do not know, but it seems that he offered some explanation in terms of observable, natural processes, because only such an explanation would have been capable of rational discussion, of being corrected and leading others to try to correct it. And this was what it did.

Thales was followed in Ionia by a series of philosophers who attempted to solve the same problem by resorting to other primary substances and various natural processes (vaporization, condensation, freezing, the separation of particles from a suspension, and so on). From Ionia, philosophic thought was carried overseas to southern Italy and Sicily, where Pythagoras (about 525) made it the basis of a secret society for scientific research, religious theorizing, and political reform; Xenophanes (also about 525) developed the old notion of an indefinite divine power into a moral monotheism, critical of idolatry and of popular legends about the gods, and Parmenides (about 475) developed the notion that a thing either is or is not, into a doctrine of two opposing worlds, one of reality, the other of appearance.

Such speculations, as they were the ultimate expression of the period's individualism, were also the most exclusive side of its upper-class culture. Any free and respectable Greek with money could enter horses at Olympia; systematic speculative thought, however, required not only leisure and education, but also intelligence. Therefore philosophy, during this period, was for the few.

For the many there was the literature of native shrewdness. Aesop, famous for the fables later attributed to him, is supposed to have been a slave in Samos during the sixth century. At the opposite pole from Aesop's common sense was a widespread literature of "revelations" under the names of legendary poets and ecstatics, notably Orpheus, teaching a fantastic mythology and claiming to prepare the soul by special rites for the dangers it would run in the afterlife. From this hodgepodge of pretentious fraud and genuine poetry, primitive superstition and profound feeling, the western world derives much of its notions of heaven and hell.

The darkest side of Greek culture during the centuries of colonization was the fact that warfare was chronic. Almost every city-state repeatedly fought with its neighbors over trivial matters. Military service was the first duty of every male citizen not utterly incapacitated, and military service usually meant hand-to-hand fighting, sticking a spear into someone while he was trying to stick a spear into you. This explains much of the Greek concern for physical culture and the constant representation of military themes in Greek art.

Hence, too, the importance of the change in tactics which occurred during the seventh century. Before that time the members of the oligarchic families were the only ones who could afford full armor; against them the lightly armed troops of the poorer citizens had little chance. But

as the growth of imports lowered the price of metal and
skill in metalworking became more common, it became
possible for a citizen of moderate means to equip himself
with a full suit of armor: helmet, breastplate, greaves,
shield, short sword, and spear. Foot soldiers thus armed
(hoplites) could form a solid wall of shields and spears
which even cavalry hesitated to attack. By the end of the
seventh century, the solid wall of hoplites became the uni-
versal and decisive military formation. The military basis
for the power of the ruling families was destroyed.

At the same time the economic basis of their security,
the expansion of Greek economy, was dwindling. By the
end of the seventh century the best spots for colonization
had already been taken; new colonies with exports to sell
had to face the competition of those already established;
natives were becoming civilized as a result of their contacts
with Greeks and were better able to drive off new settlements. More Greeks decided to stay home, and the competition within the old Greek cities became sharper. The
increase of population rapidly outdistanced both the increase of arable land and the slight improvements of agricultural technique. Consequently, increased cultivation of
the same soil gradually exhausted it, and the decline of
fertility is reflected by the increased concern for fertility
cults in the late sixth and fifth centuries, especially, in
Attica, the city's patronage of the cults of Dionysus and
Demeter. But these were not efficient soil restoratives, and
the declining yield of their lands progressively impover-
ished the peasantry. Moreover, the growth of trade had
greatly increased the wealth of the rich, who had money to
invest in ships and cargoes. The introduction of coinage had
made wealth easier to loan. Lending (at high rates of in-

terest) frequently led to foreclosure, and the debtor's person was often seized if his property failed to satisfy. The number of slaves was increased not only by this means but also by import, and competition from slave labor may have made the lot of the poor yet more difficult. The major trading cities were gradually filled with slaves, sold-out farmers, and small artisans on the verge of ruin and ready for revolt.

These men now began to find leaders, usually ambitious men from the upper class, where the frictions of life in a small city had almost always produced a complex pattern of feuds. From time to time a loser in such feuds saw the opportunity of putting himself at the head of the discontented poor and producing a revolution. When he succeeded he became a ruler of a different type from the oligarchs before him. They had ruled within the pattern of class conventions, the rudimentary constitutional laws described earlier in this chapter. The new ruler owed his power to a group anxious to see such conventions changed. He was not bound by them, and the Greeks accordingly referred to him by the non-Greek term *tyrannos*, which had previously been used to describe certain absolute rulers. The English word "tyrant" owes its connotations partly to the behavior of these tyrants, who often took advantage of their absolute power, but more to the hatred of them by the upper class from which most early Greek literature came.

Most of the big trading cities went through at least one period of tyranny in the late seventh and sixth centuries. In spite of local differences the tyrants followed a roughly uniform policy dictated by the social and economic factors which put them into power and leading to roughly uniform results. First they launched building programs—public works to improve the economic facilities and living conditions of the city, to increase its prestige and beauty, and to make work for their supporters. Harbors, aqueducts, fountains, fortifications, and temples soon stood as monuments to their rule. Next they legislated in defense of small traders, artisans, and farmers, offering even direct subsidies or tax relief to encourage certain groups. They tried to strengthen their prestige and also indulged their tastes by maintaining brilliant courts, making great displays at the games, patronizing artists and poets and other entertainers. Thus they perpetuated the more popular aspect of the oligarchic tradition. With the same concerns they patronized religion, particularly those newer forms in which the priesthoods were not monopolized by the oligarchic families, and they turned the religious festivals to further occasions of display. To finance these policies and to satisfy their followers they often expropriated and redivided the property—especially the lands—of their opponents. Such measures often made it necessary for them to maintain a corps of guards and led to the execution or exile of their more determined enemies (if this had not been a first step). Those of their enemies who could, fled to the neighboring cities and thence intrigued against them—from this time on political exiles were an important element in the instability of Greek states. Finally these intrigues would be successful, a counterrevolution would produce its crop of executions and exiles and involve the city in more plots and sufferings.

Two major states of Greece avoided this pattern: Sparta and Athens.

Sparta had been conquered by a group of Dorians rather

late in the dark ages. After the conquest the new rulers kept themselves aloof from the natives, whom they made serfs (helots). Then came the pressure of increasing population. Sparta met it, as did other Greek states, by trying to expand at the expense of her neighbors. She was unusually successful. By the late eighth century she had completely overrun the territory of Messenia and so had acquired all the southern end of the Peloponnese. That her expansion was military rather than economic may explain why her constitutional development ended with a much-modified dual monarchy. The success of the military expansion relieved the population pressure, so she did little colonizing, concentrated her strength at home, and became the greatest military power of Greece. This worried her neighbors and in the mid-seventh century they backed a revolt of Sparta's subject population, especially in Messenia, which gave the Spartans such a scare that from then on their thought was dominated by considerations of internal and external military security.

At this time military strength was coming to mean hoplite troops, and the essential of good hoplite tactics was the maintainance of that wall of shields and spears unbroken, at a run, in full armor, across irregular terrain. This required constant practice, iron discipline, and a strong sense of comradeship. These needs were seen all over Greece, but Sparta saw them with particular clarity— legend had it that the state was saved at the last moment by a drill master. Moreover, in Sparta the need was more constant and pressing than anywhere else because of the necessity of holding down the subject population, which could not be liquidated, since it did the agricultural work that fed the state. Consequently, after the revolt, over a period of more than half a century, the state was reorganized as a military camp.

Since the helots did the work, the citizens' entire lives could be devoted to public and military duties. To prevent their developing other interests they were prohibited from engaging in agriculture, business, or any craft. Money was permitted only in the form of iron spits, so cumbersome as to be practically useless. To foster comradeship and awareness of mutual interest it was arranged that most of a man's time should be spent with his military comrades; common meals in public mess halls were made compulsory; family life was reduced to a minimum; independent intellectual and artistic activity was stamped out. To prevent the development of individualism and to inculcate the patterns of behavior required by the state, boys were taken from their homes at the age of twelve and brought up in troops. Besides the training in physical exercises and music common to most Greek states, they were taught concern for their own standing in the eyes of their fellows, respect for their elders and for rules, obedience, endurance of hardship, modesty, silence, extreme brevity of speech when speech was required, military exercises, and such arts of general utility as lying and stealing. As young men, they tried out their training in the secret police, of which the principal task was to ferret out and murder any helots who might become leaders of revolt. The goal of their training, however, was the army. To make military life more attractive all other forms of life were systematically made as bare as possible, but to prevent the army from going soft the men of military age, too, were compelled to live lives of hardship. Rewards were limited to public honors which did nothing to make life more comfortable. Victors in the Olympic games, for instance, were rewarded by being assigned to the front ranks in battle. These measures were successful. Sparta became and long remained the most single-minded of the major Greek states, a military machine devoted to perpetuating itself.

The Spartans themselves not merely tolerated their home-made penal colony, but actually were proud of it. This is not surprising; the narrower a society, the more likely its members are to accept its standards as absolutely right. What is surprising is the admiration Sparta evoked elsewhere in Greece. Part of this admiration was due to its military success; more, to the recognition that Spartan life was a training for "virtue" in the "good, old-fashioned" sense—a sense which changes little from age to age because it is inculcated in childhood and the virtues which adults demand from children are relatively constant: concern for parental opinion, respect, obedience, endurance of hardship ("Stop crying!"), modesty, and silence. Deeper yet was the appeal to that side of the Greek character which was antithetical to the delight in life shown by Greek art and literature. Sparta before the great revolt had been in the forefront of the artistic and literary development, a luxurious state which drew to itself poets from Ionia and ivory and gold work from the Near East. Now, all such things were put away; the new pleasures were those of deliberate asceticism, of communal self-denial. Although self-inflicted sufferings are widespread in most societies and presumably gratify deep psychological drives, Greek society was singularly free of them and Greek religion offered them little justification. Therefore that side of the Spartan character which required them seized on prudential considerations to justify them, and what could not be excused as superstition was applauded as wisdom. But long after the prudential considerations had ceased to exist, when Rome was in full control of the Peloponnese, the Spartan tradition of asceticism was maintained. The deep root which thus perpetuated Spartan practice also explains its hold on the Greek philosophical imagination. In Sparta we stand at the chief historical fountainhead of that ascetic ideal which was to influence, through Plato's *Republic,* much western political thought, through the Stoic and Cynic schools of philosophy, the lives of innumerable individuals, and through monasticism, the whole structure of the western world.

Athens, like Sparta, began its expansion overland. At some time in the dark ages it brought all Attica under its rule, but instead of making serfs of the rest of the population it made them citizens and won their loyalty. Its territory, like Sparta's, absorbed most of the increase of its population, so it, too, had no need to colonize and, for a long while, did not. This did nothing to encourage trade, and since it had more territory to farm than did most of the trading states it was not so deeply nor so early affected as they by the economic and social crisis at the end of the seventh century.

An attempt to set up a tyranny, before 630, was probably inspired by the tyrant of neighboring Megara and failed for lack of popular support. The nobles, also, gave way gradually before popular demands. Classification of the citizens by wealth replaced classification by birth; much of the law was codified and made public shortly before 621 and a legal reform was effected in 593. Solon, who accomplished this latter, seems to have been a man of justice and moderation. At least, he satisfied nobody, was much abused during his administration and generally admired after his death. Besides passing measures for the immediate financial relief and subsequent protection of the lower classes (notably prohibition of enslavement for debt), he encouraged manufacture and trade by a series of economic measures, abolished the property requirement for participation in the meetings of the public assembly (which elected the magistrates), and reportedly constituted a final court in which the judges were a panel drawn by lot from the entire citizen body. (Among the cases which came before this court were those of ex-magistrates charged with malfeasance in office.) Finally he is said to have transferred the preparation of the assembly's agenda from an old, upper-class council to a newly created one drawn from a much wider economic group. These measures assured lower-class control of the final court and the election of magistrates; thus they laid the basis of the democratic tradition of Athens, but they did not immediately secure democracy.

Conditions continued to be difficult, and about thirty years later a war hero named Pisistratus, who had played an important part in winning one of the recurrent conflicts with Megara, became tyrant. He followed the usual policy of tyrants with unusual moderation and success, preserved the external forms of the old government, exerted himself to improve the lot of the small farmers, won for Athens a footing in the Hellespont and a share in the Black Sea trade, successfully encouraged other Attic trade, built up the city as a show place, and died peaceably in 527. His son Hippias presently lost public sympathy, but was strong enough to hold on until 510, when Spartan assistance enabled his opponents to run him out. After a brief upheaval, a new democratic regime was established under the leader-

ship of an aristocrat named Cleisthenes, and a council of
five hundred emerged as the supreme administrative authority of the state. This council soon came to be drawn by
lot from all citizens and divided for administrative purposes
into ten committees, each of which served a tenth of the
year. Above the council was the authority of the assembly
of the whole people, which retained the legislative power.
The relative simplicity of governmental problems is shown
by the fact that such machinery not only functioned, but
enabled the Athenians to survive a war with their neighbors and to conquer some territory on the mainland northeast of Attica and on the island of Euboea. So matters stood
when an ambassador from Miletus arrived in 500 to ask
help for the Ionians' revolt against the Persians.

CHAPTER III

Triumph and Tragedy

DURING the second quarter of the sixth century the Greeks of Ionia had been attacked by the Lydians, who had built up an inland kingdom in western Asia Minor and now wanted the ports along the coast. Had the Greek cities stood together they might have retained their independence. The island cities, however, which felt themselves safer, were lax in helping those on the mainland; Miletus, chief of the mainland towns, made a separate peace; the smaller places went down one by one. By 550 all were in Lydian hands. In the 540's Lydia itself was overwhelmed by Persia, and the Greek cities on the coast passed under Persian control. For thirty years thereafter the Persians were occupied in strengthening their eastern frontier, conquering Egypt, and suppressing revolts. Then, in 512, they marched against the Scythians, a nomadic people who at that time ranged the western and northern shores of the Black Sea. The campaign ended in Persian withdrawal after heavy losses. A dozen years later the Ionian cities revolted. They sent to the other Greek states for help and got twenty ships from Athens and five from Eretria.

Consequently, after putting down the Ionian revolt in the years following 500, the Persians moved against main-

land Greece. In 492 Thrace and Macedonia were subjugated, and more might have been attempted had not the
Persian fleet been wrecked off Mount Athos. In 490 a new
fleet was sent directly across the Aegean. Eretria was
burned and its people carried off captive. Athens was to be
next. Hippias, the former tyrant, was with the Persian fleet;
his partisans were expected to rise against the Athenian
government and help the Persians restore him. The Persians
landed on the east coast of Attica at the plain of Marathon.
By prompt action the Athenians, with the help of their
neighbors from the little city of Plataea, defeated the landing force before any uprising could take place. The Persian
fleet then sailed around the Attic peninsula, hoping to reach
Athens before the army should return, but the army returned at once and was ready for them. Therefore they did
not attempt a landing, but sailed back to Asia Minor. Any
thought of a further expedition was broken off by the death
of the Great King, as the Persian ruler was called. His suc-
cessor, Xerxes, had to spend the first years of his reign
suppressing revolts. Accordingly the Greeks had ten years'
respite.

These ten years saw a great increase in the importance of
Athens. The policies of Solon and Pisistratus had already
given her a chief place among the trading cities. Her defeat
of the Persians had increased her military prestige and self-
confidence. Her self-confidence now got a shock when her
chronic war with the rival trading city of Aegina, on an
island just across the Saronic Gulf, went badly. Then came
the discovery of rich deposits of silver near the tip of the
Attic peninsula, and a politician named Themistocles persuaded the city to use its new wealth in building up its
navy. Just at this time a new type of warship was coming

into general use. Where the old warships had been rowed
by fifty oars, the new ones—triremes—had a hundred and
seventy, arranged in three banks. Besides their rowers, they
carried twenty-five or thirty officers and hands and could
also carry some marines. Since Athens now replaced her
old warships by triremes, when the next Persian attack
came she was able to contribute not only more ships than
all the other Greek states put together but faster and more
heavily manned ships, too. She had achieved a pre-eminence
on sea comparable to that of Sparta on land.

The Persian attack came in 480. It was a carefully
planned campaign to conquer all Greece and was perhaps
the largest military operation the world had ever seen. Yet
the immense Persian army and navy which bore down on
Greece was only one jaw of a gigantic pair of pincers. The
other jaw, originating from Carthage, the great African
colony of Persia's Phoenician subjects, moved from the
southwest against the Greeks of Sicily. The figures given
in Greek reports for the Persian and Carthaginian forces
are fantastic, but it is not impossible that they may together have involved three hundred thousand men. On the
eastern front the Persian preparations were on a scale ap-
propriate to the numbers involved: a pontoon bridge, using
boats for pontoons, was built across the Hellespont, a ship
canal was dug through the isthmus connecting Mount
Athos to the mainland, stores of food and equipment were
prepared in Thrace and Macedonia.

These preparations made the Greeks aware of their common danger and persuaded some of them to act together
in self-defense. Some, but by no means all. Delphi was pro-
Persian (the prudent interpreters of Apollo were more used
to tell of miracles than to expect them). Thessaly and its

hinterland went over to the Persian side as soon as the Great King's army approached. The Greeks of Crete refused to participate in the common defense, and so on. But Sparta, Athens, Corinth, Thebes, and some two dozen of the minor city-states did join their forces under Spartan leadership.

A first attempt to stop the Persians was made at the pass of Thermopylae. Here the Spartan King, Leonidas, was posted with a Greek force of at first almost seven thousand, ultimately only fourteen hundred men. These held up the entire Persian army for a week by heroic and eventually suicidal resistance. After Thermopylae the Spartans made no further effort to defend either Central Greece or Attica, but devoted themselves to fortifying the Isthmus of Corinth. Thebes, the largest city of Boeotia, went over to the Persians. In Athens, the majority of the citizens fled, mostly to the island of Salamis, where the Greek fleet had gathered. The Persian army marched almost unopposed through Boeotia and Attica, occupied Athens, overcame a few fanatics who tried to hold the Acropolis, and destroyed the city. The Persian fleet meanwhile rounded the point of Attica, sailed up the Saronic Gulf, and anchored off Athens, blocking the southern entrance to the straits which separate Salamis from the mainland. Themistocles now persuaded the Greek fleet in the straits of Salamis to await the Persian attack there, where the Persians would get least benefit from their superiority in numbers. He also tricked the Persians into blocking the other entrance to the straits, thus forcing the Greeks to stay there anyhow. In the ensuing battle so many Persian ships were destroyed that Xerxes withdrew the remainder to guard his route of return across the Hellespont.

At the same time the Carthaginian invasion of Sicily was routed by Gelon, tyrant of Syracuse, at the battle of Himera, and Greek control of most of the island for another seventy years was secured.

Salamis was fought late in September. The military season was then over for the year, and Xerxes returned to Asia Minor for the winter but left in Greece a large army, which wintered in Thessaly. The Great King may have intended to come back in the spring, but a revolt in Babylonia prevented this and the army left in Greece went unsupported. It was defeated in the summer at Plataea by the united Greek land force under the Spartan regent, Pausanias. Only a remnant got back to Asia Minor.

In the same year as the battle of Plataea (479) the remainder of the Persian fleet in Asia Minor was caught on shore by the Greeks at Mount Mycale, just north of Miletus, and destroyed.

After these defeats the Persians could no longer hold subject the Greek cities on the Aegean coast. Many revolted at once. But others required outside help to throw off their Persian garrisons. And even those which regained their freedom at once could not hope to keep it unless the power of European Greece were alert to protect them against further Persian attacks.

However, most of the little places which had banded together to fight off the Persians had neither mind nor means to become involved in long operations on the other side of the Aegean. Even Sparta, the official leader of the league, was reluctant to send her men so far from home. The helots were always a domestic threat, and foreign service might corrupt the men, undermining their Spartan discipline. When she did send out Pausanias, he was corrupted.

Yet worse, his authoritarian behavior made him insupportable to the allies. He had to be recalled.

Athens, on the other hand, had ties of kinship with the Ionian cities of Asia Minor. As the chief trading city of the Aegean, she wanted to ring the sea with friendly ports. She particularly wanted to end Persian control over access to the Black Sea and its trade. She had the ships necessary for the overseas war. She had a ruling class used to the ways of the world and able to organize the co-operative effort which the circumstances required. Finally, under Themistocles' leadership, she had rebuilt her own fortifications and fortified a rocky promontory, the Piraeus, so as to make a group of defensible harbors. This made her independent of her mainland neighbors and free to follow her own policies overseas.

Accordingly, when Sparta abdicated leadership, Athens assumed it. In 478 or 477 she organized what is known as the Delian league. Each member was to contribute, according to ability, ships, and men or money. There was to be a common treasury, the ancient Ionian shrine of Apollo on Delos, and a common council, meeting there. Each of the allied states was to have a representative and a vote. Athens, by far the largest contributor, was sure of preeminence in the council and of the military command.

The scheme was successful beyond expectation. Liberation of the coastal cities of Thrace and Asia Minor went on apace, and the league increased the number of its members. Since military service was burdensome, more and more of the members preferred to substitute money payments. The Athenians undertook the military burden and paid for it with the money contributed by their allies, who thus built up the Athenian navy while themselves losing the habit of self-defense. Presently the league was able to turn its attention to other matters. Island cities which had sided with the Persians during the invasion could now be punished, and this could be profitable. Pirate strongholds could be cleaned out in the common interest, especially in the interest of the major trading city, which also planted colonies on the islands thus made vacant. Eventually came the day when a member of the league got tired of contributing and decided to withdraw. This was Naxos. Naxos was subjugated by the Athenian forces about 470, and the allies of the Delian league found themselves effectively subject states of an Athenian empire.

At home, however, Athens was becoming more democratic. Before the Persian war the chief executive officers of the state had come to be chosen by lot, but so many incompetents were thus selected that the allotted offices lost their powers and the most influential positions in the state came to be those which remained elective because they could not safely be entrusted to fools. A board of ten generals was annually elected, and commands in particular campaigns were voted to one or another as occasion arose. Besides military affairs the board came to have charge of the grain supply, the state finances, and foreign policy. But even successful generals were not safe from the passion or stupidity of the people. Any unpopular official action was apt to be followed by accusation and trial before a court composed of hundreds or even thousands of members chosen by lot. Besides formal prosecution, there was a device known as "ostracism" by which the man who got the most votes in a general unpopularity contest was banished for ten years. To get a man ostracized, any slander would suffice. Themistocles, who had done so much to make the city powerful and save it from the Persians, was ostracized and then, in his absence, condemned to death on a charge of conspiracy with the Persians; he narrowly escaped capture and ended his days as a pensioner of the Great King. Next it was the turn of the next most competent general, Cimon. He had conquered a series of outposts for the Athenian empire, subjected a number of Athens' reluctant allies, and defeated a Persian expedition which set out in the 460's to re-establish Persian influence in the Aegean; but he was on good terms with the Spartans. When Sparta was devastated by earthquake in 464 and then threatened by a rising of the Messenian helots, he persuaded the Athenians to send an expeditionary force to help put down the revolt. The Spartans came to suspect that the Athenians of this force were plotting against them; accordingly they asked the force to leave. Athens reacted to the request by ostracizing Cimon and siding with the Messenians. When it was finally settled that the Messenians should leave Sparta, Athens gave them a home at Naupactus, where they strengthened her hold on the Gulf of Corinth and her ability to bottle up, if necessary, Corinth's trade with the west.

Cimon had been the leader of the conservative party. His ostracism was largely procured by two younger men of the popular party for whom it left the stage open, Ephialtes and Pericles. Ephialtes was not likely to be ostracized. He was now murdered and the murder was generally blamed on his conservative opponents. It left Pericles in power.

Pericles remained in power from 461 to 430. His policy was determined by two factors, the democracy and the empire of Athens. These two factors were complementary: the democracy provided the popular support and dynamism for the empire, the empire provided the money and emotional outlets for the democracy. To maintain the empire it was necessary, first of all, to maintain the navy. This required rowers. The rowers came largely from the lowest class of citizens. They had to be paid well, as rowing was both hard work and skilled work, and they had to be satisfied with the general policy of the state. Therefore the state must be a democracy, and because it was a democracy the lowest class was interested in maintenance of the empire which assured it of employment and of political importance. Further, to maintain the empire it was desirable to have supporters in the subject states ("the allies"). Support was not likely to come in these states from the upper classes, who were often commercial rivals of the Athenians and always taxed to pay the tribute to pay for the navy. Therefore Athens intervened in the domestic affairs of her allies on behalf of the lower classes. This intervention was not merely an expression of preference for the democratic forms of government she imposed. At best it was an attempt to base the empire on lower-class support abroad as it was based at home; at worst it was an application of the principle, divide and rule. Thus Athens assumed among the Greek city-states the role formerly played by the tyrant within the Greek city: she protected the poor against the oligarchs; the poor supported her and enabled her to act without concern for customary obligations. When her enemies spoke of her as a tyrant city, they intended the term to be accurate as well as abusive; Pericles himself is represented as telling the Athenians that they held their rule as a tyranny and could not safely relinquish it.

These facts explain the policy of Pericles. He was not himself a tyrant. He did not set himself above the laws of his own city; he was regularly elected, year after year, to the board of generals; he met considerable opposition and met it by legal means. But the policies dictated by the position of his city were the policies of the tyrants.

First there were direct grants to the poor: Pericles instituted payments to enable poor citizens to attend the theaters and to serve in the courts—this altered the temper of the courts, by making service more attractive to the poor than to the rich. Subsequent provisions for the transfer of cases from "allied" cities to Athens increased the amount of employment for the Athenians, brought to the city many litigants who had to spend money there, and subjected the wealthy men of other states to the jurisdiction of the democratic Athenian courts.

Next there was seizure of property. Seizure of the property of "allies" who revolted was a well-established policy of the Delian league; under Pericles it was carried on in many instances; he himself took charge of the suppression of Samos. The common fund of the league was an obvious opportunity for seizure: it was transferred from Delos to Athens in 454 and the meetings of the council were discontinued. Besides this, from 461 to 446 Pericles followed a policy of military expansion in mainland Greece. Megara, northern Euboea, and points along the Gulf of Corinth were seized, and Athenian control was temporarily extended over Boeotia. At the same time, however, he attempted expansion to the east. An intermittent war was carried on for the liberation of the Greeks of Cyprus. Dor, on the Palestinian coast, was seized and used as a base for an expedition to Egypt to support a rebellion against the Persians there. This overextended the Athenian power. The

Egyptian expedition ended in disaster, Dor was lost, and Pericles chose to sacrifice the Greeks of Cyprus. The Peace of Callias in 449 left them to Persia, but assured Athens of undisturbed control in the Aegean and thus of a free hand in Greece itself. But the sacrifice was in vain, for it was followed by defeats in Greece and the loss of Boeotia and Megara. A "thirty-years' peace" with Sparta in 446 put an end to this phase of Pericles' policy. He found a substitute in colonization, first in the Thracian Chersonese, in northern Euboea and Naxos in 447, and then in other Aegean islands, in Macedonia, Thrace, southern Italy, the districts around the Black Sea, and so on. Thus he seized land for the city's supporters, especially the poorer Athenian citizens, and the empire was strengthened by military and mercantile outsettlements.

Protection of artisans and encouragement of trade were characteristics of the same policy. Pericles' military program gave employment to Athenian metalworkers, shipbuilders, and so on. The Egyptian expedition was undertaken in hope of capturing the trade of Egypt. Colonization in southern Italy and treaties with Italian and Sicilian cities were intended to increase Athenian trade in that area at the expense of Corinth. An expedition to the Black Sea extended commercial relations as well as colonization there. (The region was important to Athens as a source of salt fish and grain. Cheap food for the poor of the city was a primary goal of this policy: it helped the lower classes, on whom the regime rested, and it weakened the aristocratic opposition, of which the core was Attic landowners, whose incomes depended on the prices of the products of their lands.) These far-flung trading interests were tied together by standardization of coinage: most of the subject states were prohibited from continuing to mint their own currencies and required to use Athenian coin instead.

Finally, the program of building for the strengthening and glorification of Athens was also characteristic of tyrannical policy. The first (458), and politically the most important, step in this was the building of "the long walls" to connect the city with the Piraeus and prevent its being cut off from the sea by a land attack. This was the basis of Pericles' military confidence. The last step of the program and that most important to the arts was the building of the architectural complex on the Acropolis and especially of its crowning structure, the Parthenon. This, like his program of colonization, Pericles began in 447, when his military schemes were failing. Partly, the new building gave the citizens something to talk about and distracted their attention from the failure, partly it increased their pride and delight in the city and thus their loyalty to Pericles, partly it made work for the artisans whom the suspension of military activities would leave idle. This last consideration was decisive. The work was paid for from the funds contributed by the members of the Delian league for defense against the Persians. Pericles' opponents objected that "Greece will think it a shameful insult and a conspicuous example of tyranny if those funds, which it was compelled to contribute for the war, are openly used by us to gild the city and paint it up like a strumpet" (the marble sculptures and decoration of the temples were painted) "hung around with precious stones and statues and million-dollar temples." Pericles, however, persuaded the people:

that they owed no accounting for the money to the allies, since they did the fighting for them and kept off the barbarians, while the allies contributed no horse nor ship nor hoplite, but only money. Money is not the property of those who give it, but of those who receive it, if they provide the services for which it is given them. Moreover, now that the city has been sufficiently equipped with the necessities for the war, its funds may properly be used for these new plans which if carried out will yield eternal glory and immediate prosperity, since they require all sorts of labor and create various needs which put every skill to work, keep every hand busy, and employ almost the whole city, at once adorning and supporting itself [Plutarch, *Pericles*, XII].

The Parthenon made work from 447–432. The rest of the Acropolis was still far from completion at Pericles' death in 429. Other temples, too, were built, especially the shrine of Demeter and Persephone, the goddesses of the Earth and the Underworld, at Eleusis. There was considerable building of markets, harbors, and fortifications, and also for aesthetic purposes, notably a large music hall at Athens. Pericles' patronage of the theater, by instituting payments to enable the poor to attend, has already been mentioned. As the tyrants sought to increase their prestige by maintaining brilliant courts, so Athens was made the center not only of the naval and financial power but also of the artistic and intellectual life of the Greek world. Where formerly there had been many small centers, each with its own intellectual and artistic originality, now there was Athens and there were the provinces. The sun was risen and had eclipsed the stars.

The "thirty years' peace" with Sparta was unusually suc-

cessful, as peace treaties go: it ran for fifteen years, from
446 to 431. The outbreak of the Peloponnesian War in 431
resulted from a variety of causes. Athens had renounced
aggression in mainland Greece, but was still on the ag-
gressive abroad. The objects of her aggression were her
chief competitors in trade, Corinth and Megara. She had
recently tried to compel one Corinthian colony, Potidaea,
to break off connections with the mother city; she was
supporting another, Corcyra, in its revolt. She now passed
a decree prohibiting the Megarians to use any ports be-
longing to Athens or its allies. This would practically ban
them from the Aegean. In their consequent hostility,
Corinth and Megara were joined by Thebes, which wanted
to unite Boeotia under its control and was prevented from
doing so by the Athenian alliance with Plataea. Corinth
now appealed to Sparta. The Spartans were of two minds.
On the one hand, they saw their traditional pre-eminence
threatened by the continually increasing Athenian empire;
on the other, they were reluctant to undertake anything
which would draw them out of their shell. They were now
persuaded to participate in sending Athens an ultimatum.
In Athens, Pericles was not averse to the war. The stories
that he precipitated it to cover domestic difficulties are
certainly exaggerations, but it may have served such purposes incidentally. Certainly it would give business to his
supporters, the artisans and merchants, and would open a
wide range of opportunities for pirate enterprise to the
democratic navy; it would ruin the big Attic landowners
and would demonstrate the relative unimportance of the
army, which was a stronghold of upper-class feeling. (Since
the soldiers were required to provide their own armor, only
those of at least moderate means could serve.) Moreover,

he thought that if Athens yielded to this ultimatum she would soon be presented with another and yet another and finally, when weakened, would have to fight anyhow in self-defense, whereas if she fought at once she would lose little and might gain a great deal. So the war came.

Neither side had any plan for fighting it effectively. The Spartan strategy was merely to march into Attica each summer, do what damage they could, and march back. Pericles seems to have ordered his navy to pick up whatever it could along the coasts, a strategy which hurt Sparta even less than Sparta hurt Athens. As for the population of Attica, Pericles had foreseen that when the Spartans came it could take refuge inside the city's fortifications, but he seems never to have thought of how the refugees would be taken care of. They were left to camp in vacant lots and temples and at corners of the city walls. The sanitary consequences of such statesmanship must have been breathtaking. Amazingly, the plague did not strike until the second summer. Then it carried off perhaps a third of the population. Pericles died in the following year (429), but the men who succeeded him in power had no more idea than he did of how to conduct an effective war, so the stalemate went on. Finally in 425 more serious developments began: an Athenian commander operating off the west coast of the Peloponnese chanced to seize a headland there. He found it an ideal base from which to organize subversive activities among the helots of Sparta. This so frightened the Spartans that they tried to drive him out, failed to do so, and lost 420 first-class troops in the process. To them this was a major loss, for military comradeship and the general austerity of Spartan life had diminished their birth rate, and every man mattered. The next year a Spartan general had the idea of taking an army to Chalcidice to liberate Athens' un-willing allies there. The allies welcomed him, and he was presently able to take Amphipolis in eastern Macedonia. Amphipolis was important—it controlled communications along the coast, a trade route to the north, and an area rich in gold and silver and timber and tar for the fleet. Holding it, the Spartans were able to threaten the whole north Aegean coast. Thus the war began to hurt both Athens and Sparta, so an armistice was arranged in 423, and peace was concluded in 421.

This "First" Peloponnesian War thus accomplished nothing. Perhaps its most important event—after the plague at Athens—was the failure of the Athenian general Thucydides to save Amphipolis from his Spartan opponent. This resulted in his exile from Athens, which enabled him to devote the leisure, relative objectivity, and analytical hindsight of an exiled general to the composition of a history of the war so penetrating that it marks the beginning of modern historical thought.

Because the war had not struck at vital areas, it had not changed the social and economic structure which produced it. Athens was still the tyrant city, compelled by the same economic needs to follow the same policy as before. Sparta was still Sparta, with its narrow military aristocracy equally distrustful at home and abroad, but more resentful than ever of Athens' challenge to its pre-eminence. The minor states were even less reconciled: Corinth, for instance, never accepted the peace. Therefore it is not unreasonable to treat the "Second" Peloponnesian War, which officially began in 414, as a continuation of the first.

Again events were precipitated by the imperialism of Athens and particularly by her attempt to take over territory which had formerly been Corinthian. Syracuse was originally a Corinthian colony. Though long independent, it retained an affection for the mother city which probably accounted for much of Corinth's continued importance in trade with the west. Athens, therefore, found a pretext for an expedition in 415 to conquer Syracuse: 137 ships, over 25,000 sailors, 7,150 land troops—and 30 horses. (The cavalry was made up of the citizens rich enough to keep horses for military purposes; it was anything but a bulwark of democracy, and horses were difficult to transport.) This was by no means the total strength of Athens, but it represented a great effort and was deemed sufficient to conquer one of the largest cities in the Greek world.

Unfortunately for the expedition, its most energetic general, Alcibiades, left behind him a wide circle of exasperated enemies. He was a wealthy, brilliant, and scandalously beautiful young man who had been the ward of Pericles, had fallen in love with Socrates, and had so distinguished himself by his public speaking, his race horses, and his democratic politics that he was suspected by many of plotting to become tyrant, but by more, of lacking proper respect for the gods, the laws, and his elders, including themselves. Just before the Syracusan expedition sailed, a number of the statues of the god Hermes, which displayed their erect phalli in the streets of Athens, were mutilated. Rumor blamed Alcibiades and his friends; he was said also to have given parties at which the guests were entertained by parodies of the sacred mysteries performed at Eleusis. His enemies waited until the expedition, containing most of his supporters, had sailed, and then sent an order for him to return to stand trial—before a court which would be made up largely of men from the older generation. He preferred flight to death and fled to Sparta. This left the expedition in the hands of less energetic and capable men; it bogged down in besieging Syracuse and eventually found itself besieged instead. In 413, Athens, by severe sacrifice, sent another expedition of 73 ships, about 14,000 sailors, 5,000 heavy infantry, and an unspecified number of light-armed troops. Even these new troops were not sufficient to capture the city. It soon became apparent that the whole expedition would have to withdraw, and had better do so at once. Just then, however, came an eclipse of the moon. Most of the Athenians took this as an omen and urged the generals to delay sailing. The ranking general, acting on the advice of his prophets, refused to move for thrice nine days. During this time the Syracusans blocked the Athenian ships in the harbor. The Athenians were unable to escape, and everything left of both expeditions was lost.

Meanwhile in Greece, on Alcibiades' advice, Sparta had resumed the war in 414. Now it established a fortress in the north of Attica, to serve as a base for year-round raiding and a refuge for runaway slaves. Between raids and runaways the produce of Attic farms and mines was largely lost. When the expedition to Syracuse was destroyed in 413, the Syracusans and their Sicilian allies and fleet came into the war on the Spartan side. In 412 Persia entered the war on the Spartan side. At the same time most of the "allies" of Athens along the Ionian coast revolted. After these disasters the democratic party in Athens was discredited. In 411, under pressure from elements of the army, the constitution was remodeled on oligarchic lines, and the new rulers attempted to reach an agreement with Sparta. But this the people were not ready to accept; the people had the navy on their side, and the navy had a firm base on Samos, where compulsory democracy had been established by Pericles and was maintained by murdering the remnants of the upper class. From Samos the navy reconquered much of the empire. Alcibiades was recalled as supreme general, democracy was restored in Athens, and Spartan offers of peace were refused. But the new Athenian democracy was immoderate by nature and exasperated by circumstance. It was no firm base for any military program. Alcibiades, after a naval defeat, was deprived of his command, retired to a fortress in the Thracian Chersonese, fled thence to the Persians, and by them was put to death. The generals who succeeded him won some victories but could not retain the support of the assembly. Moreover Athens was nearing exhaustion, while the Spartans now had Persian money; they could always hire new rowers and build new fleets. In 405 the last Athenian fleet was destroyed. In 404 Athens surrendered to the Spartans, and Samos was reduced by siege a few months later.

The Athenian empire thus rose and fell within seventy-five years (478–404). It was the shortest lived of the famous empires of the ancient world. It was also the tiniest. At its greatest extent it comprised little more than a bit of southeastern Greece, most of the islands of the Aegean, and the cities along its northern and eastern coasts, a scattering of places on the southern coast of Asia Minor, around the Black Sea and its approaches, and up the western coast of Greece, and a colony in southern Italy. In military strength it could muster at sea about 300 ships, manned by about 60,000 men, while on land it had slightly over 30,000 troops, of which, however, half were reserves. Neither the land troops nor the men on the ships were all

Athenian citizens; citizens probably accounted for 50,000, at most, of the 90,000. Now military service was compulsory for all citizens physically capable of it, from the ages of twenty to forty-nine inclusive, and the number of citizens over this age was probably not great: ancient medical science was such that old men were rare enough to be respected. Therefore the total citizen body of Athens probably numbered, at the very most, about 60,000. This would imply an equal number of adult women and over twice as many children no longer infants. (Mortality was high even among adolescents, and among infants it was probably enormous.) Then there were slaves: the poor citizen who rowed in the navy probably had no slave, the small farmer or shopkeeper had two or three, the rich sometimes had thousands (hired out for labor). A slave population somewhat larger than the number of citizens is not improbable. Finally there was a large body of resident aliens who enjoyed some legal protection but not the rights of citizens. (They were important in trade, especially in the grain trade, and as contractors and craftsmen in local business; they paid taxes and were liable to military service.) If they numbered 30,000 this number should be quadrupled to allow for their wives and children. In all, then, the population of Attica was less than half a million, of which the most part was concentrated in Athens. And it must be emphasized that the figures above are maximal.

Yet in Athens, small as it was, were concentrated, during the brief span of the Athenian empire, the achievements and the conflicts, the triumph and the tragedy, of Greek civilization.

The economic achievement which made the civilization possible was the development of the trading network of

Greek cities, from Spain to the Caucasus. This immense extension of civic and civilized life, of demands and markets and available materials, had been the work of the eighth, seventh, and sixth centuries. Athens, in the fifth century, organized much of it, bound it together by a uniform currency and a more intensive trade, and concentrated the variety of the products and the bulk of the profits in one great city. In this city, therefore, the civic and civilized life of Greece reached its acme. Here for the first time were the people and the power which made possible new achievements and gave greater significance to whatever was done.

Take city government, for example. Other cities had been governed democratically. But Athens was the center of the world. That in Athens in its greatness the people elected their own officers, maintained their own courts, taxed themselves, determined their foreign policy, and, in a word, exercised final control over every aspect of their own government—this was the great example of democracy in operation which influenced political thought throughout antiquity and inspired the democratic revolutionists of the eighteenth and nineteenth centuries. But this civic achievement had to be paid for: every district had to have its governor, secretary, treasurer, priest, herald (town crier), and so on; courts had to be made up, and hundreds of judge-jurors were required for each; the Assembly had to be attended; the Council of Five Hundred had to be filled; so did the other offices of the state (and it has been estimated that at any given moment there were no less than fourteen hundred persons occupying official posts). Performance of official duties took time. The poor could not afford it, nor the middle class be persuaded to it unless they were paid for their services. So the economic and imperial expansion of Athens and the maintenance of her democratic government went hand in hand.

A similar relationship existed between the growth of the city and the development of civilized life—the life of leisure and elegance, of refined amusements, privacy, and reflective thought. All these aspects of civilization had been anticipated in the Greek cities of the sixth century and before, in the developments of archaic art and architecture, of the festivals and games, of lyric poetry, and of Ionian philosophy. But except for the public buildings and the festivals, they had been chiefly for the aristocrats. The economic development of Athens and the exploitation of her empire now afforded a modicum of wealth and leisure to a middle class of perhaps twenty thousand of Athens' citizens, their wives, and families. These, concentrated in the one city, create a new sort of demand, for a more economical elegance and for the cheaper luxuries (including individualism and reflective thought).

This new demand is everywhere apparent. The artifacts of everyday life, chairs and beds and tables, acquire a new elegance of line and an economical simplicity which itself is elegant. There is evidence of increasing resort by all classes of citizens to the gymnasia built and maintained by public funds—and a gymnasium was not merely a place for exercise, but a center of political, erotic, and intellectual life. There was an increasing concern for women and their problems; a new softness and delicacy, especially in funerary sculpture and many artifacts, probably reflect feminine taste. Most important of all is the increasing emphasis on artistic, intellectual, and moral elements in the festivals.

Here again a sharp contrast cannot be made. The games had not been wholly upper-class assemblies, though the

members of the oligarchic families could best afford to go
to them and undoubtedly set their tone. Nor had they remained without intellectual and artistic content: contests
in music, which included the singing of original lyric
poems, had been introduced at the Pythian games, and
celebration of the victors was often an occasion for composition and singing of new lyrics. Most of the odes of
Pindar, the greatest of the lyric poets after Sappho, were
written for such occasions and derive their power from the
peculiarly Greek realization of the union of youth and
beauty and triumph as a moment of divinity in the life of
a young man who soon (being a man) will die. But when
Pindar himself died in 438, he had outlived his world. Since
the middle of the sixth century the games had been rivaled
by the development of the civic festivals which were more
easily accessible to the lower classes. Now, with the fifth
century, the January and March festivals of Dionysus, one
of the gods most worshiped by the peasants, were developed into a new sort of contest and came to provide the
classic occasions and supreme forms for original poetic
composition.

The forms were tragedy and comedy. Significantly, they
developed in Athens. Pisistratus, who knew what his supporters wanted, introduced the March festival to the city
and established a temple for the god and an adjacent danc-
ing floor, where the dramatic performances took place, on
the southern slope of the Acropolis. Cleisthenes, concerned
to get popular support after the expulsion of the family
of Pisistratus, patronized the festivals yet further. How the
original cult of the god developed so as to include classic
tragedy and comedy is a matter of dispute, but there is no
doubt that the classic drama was part of a religious cere-

mony. So were the contests in the games, and it is typical of the Greek love of contests and individualism that the dramatic festivals were also made contests: plays by three or more poets were presented at each and a winner chosen. It is yet more typical of Athenian democracy that the cost of producing the plays—like the cost of fitting out and manning the warships, and other extraordinary state expenses—should have been allocated by popular or governmental appointment to outstandingly wealthy citizens. Thus by special taxation of the rich the whole citizen body was able to enjoy the greatest literature, music, and dramaturgy of the age. Ranging from scathing political satire to penetrating psychological analysis and exquisite lyric poetry, from the most outrageous burlesque to the most profound theological speculation, the Attic drama of the fifth century is the supreme example of this new, civic and civilized life, in which the exclusive achievements of the earlier culture were further developed and by development made accessible to the citizen body as a whole.

It is the achievement of this new life which Pericles (if Thucydides reports him true) chose to celebrate in his speech at the funeral of those dead who fell in the first year of the Peloponnesian War. He said, in substance: These men are to be praised for what they loved and died for—not our political greatness alone, but the constitution from which it has arisen. That constitution is called democratic because it favors not the few, but the many. Yet it affords equal justice to all and advances men according to their capacities, not their social standing. It leaves individuals free to do as they like in their private lives, yet compels their observance not only of the civil and criminal laws, but also of the unwritten laws of decency. Moreover, we have

provided many relaxations: we celebrate games and sacrifices all the year round, and in the elegance of our homes
we enjoy a daily delight which drives out grief. Besides
this, the greatness of the city brings to us the pleasant
things of all other countries. Therefore we do not expel
strangers nor fear spies, since we trust not in stratagems,
but in our own willingness to work. Similarly in education
we do not resort to laborious drilling from childhood on,
but we get satisfactory results. We combine love of beauty
with economy, and love of wisdom with manliness. We
blame not poverty, but laziness; and we expect a citizen
not only to manage his own affairs, but also to be an
adequate judge of political questions, for we think discussion not a hindrance to action, but a prerequisite for it.
In a word, our city as a whole is the school of Greece, and,
to speak of the individual Athenian, I think that among us
the average man is able to address himself adequately to
more different problems, more easily, and, above all, with
more *savoir faire* than anywhere else in the world. That
these claims are not mere words is shown by the power
which our city has attained. Such is the Athens for which
these men died. She is what they made her. You, their sur-
vivors, must behold her power at work day by day and
likewise become her lovers.

The confidence of this speech is based on Pericles' political experience. He had observed his people, he knew what
they wanted and what would seem to them to justify their
losses in the war. Glory and Athens? Of course. But also
the new private life, the individual liberty, and the new
things to do with it, things which had never before been
available to the middle-class man. These made Athens what
it was; these were its true glory. He was aware of what

could be said against them: as a politician he knew how
ignorance and personal interest could vent themselves in
the Assembly. He must have known better than anyone
else what Athens paid for amateur administration. He was
a friend of writers and philosophers, and his mistress,
Aspasia, was a brilliant courtesan from Miletus. Aspasia and
a number of the intellectuals of his circle were prosecuted
for impiety, and he must have known what the conserva-
tives were saying about the demoralization of the city by
the neglect and criticism of old ways and the introduction
of new customs and ideas. But he looked at the facts and
began his speech by stating that individualism did not
threaten either the enforcement of civil and criminal law
or the maintenance of common decency. Against it he saw
superstition and timidity; for it he saw the beauty, joy,
and power, which sprang from the new way of life, and
he based his confidence on those.

In this love of beauty, this courage to grasp at joy and
power and risk the consequences, but also in his clear observation of facts and his common sense, he was typical of
his city and his age.

In the graphic and plastic arts naturalism, based on observation, slowly but steadily increased. The purpose of the
arts, however, was still the common-sense one of creating,
decorating, and representing beautiful things. To the
common-sense mind it is obvious that ugly and distressing
objects are not to be represented in art. If the decoration
of a temple requires the representation of a battle, for example, wounds and suffering may be indicated in subordi-
nate parts of the composition, but as a whole art is to
represent objects at their most beautiful, as they are, but
also as they should be. The master of this style was Pericles'

friend Phidias, whose genius raised him above the rank of craftsman, to which most Greek artists were relegated by their contemporaries. Phidias was in charge of the sculpture of the Parthenon and after its completion in 432 went to Olympia, where he made a famous gold and ivory statue of Zeus. As a familiar of Pericles' circle he must have been in touch with contemporary philosophy, and what he thought his deities represented is a matter for speculation. But the beauty of his work is undoubted. Of the Zeus it was said that if a man who had suffered every sorrow were to stand before it he would forget all the griefs and troubles of human life. At the other end of the social scale the decorators of pottery show the same characteristics as Phidias. Common sense reminded them that the grotesque would sell, and the range of their subjects is considerably larger than that of Phidian sculpture. But for the most part they drew to beautify and they drew the beautiful. At the same time, their work shows increasing naturalism, facilitated by the change from black- to red-figure technique, which meant that the details of the figures, instead of being incised on silhouettes, could now be painted. As in sculpture, the gain in naturalism was paid for by some loss of force and simplicity.

Similar development characterizes the history of the literature. The essential difference between the drama and the choral poetry from which it probably developed is that the drama attempts a more naturalistic presentation of the myths which the choral poetry merely sang and danced. Within the history of the drama itself there is also a clear progression toward naturalism. Of the three tragedians from whose work some plays have survived, Aeschylus, who wrote from about 490 to 456, is concerned chiefly with the theological bases of conflicts of justice and law, his characters, even when they are human beings, are primarily the representatives of the conflicting supernatural powers and speak with superhuman force and grandeur. In Sophocles, active from 468 to 406, similar conflicts are studied, but from the side of man; the interest lies in their impact on human character. In Euripides, from 455 to 406, character study becomes an end in itself, and an interest in psychopathology appears, to anticipate the studies of old age and deformity in later hellenistic art. After Euripides comes Aristophanes, 427–385, the one fifth-century comedian from whom we have complete plays. His work combines naturalism, a delight in the grotesque and a different sort of idealization—satirical exaggerations of unequaled verve. These phenomena in poetry were paralleled by the more important development of prose as a vehicle of literature. In the histories of Herodotus, who died about 429, we have the first preserved work by a Greek writer who disregards the conventional requirements of verse and sets out to tell in his own language a plain story of what reportedly happened.

This development of naturalism in art and literature is only one aspect of a general development of a new way of thought, which vies with the new way of life described above as Athens' most important contribution to the history of the world. This new way of thought had been anticipated in the Ionian philosophy of the sixth century, but Athens carried it further and transformed it from the peculiarity of a few speculative thinkers to a characteristic shaping every aspect of the city's intellectual and much of its practical life.

Ionian philosophy had begun with the attempt to explain

the origin of the world by analogies from observable material processes—condensation, rarefaction, and the like. From this it had gone on to rational criticism of its theories and hence to a new awareness that thought is systematic, that ideas imply hypotheses which must be tested and have consequences which must be faced. The naturalistic and systematic way of thought was now extended by common sense to more practical questions than the creation of the world. In medicine, Hippocrates is remembered as having demanded that the body be studied as a whole and its pathological conditions described by reference to all relevant circumstances. In historical writing Thucydides followed up the rambling narrative of Herodotus with a closely knit work expressing his concept of history as a structure of interlocking effects-becoming-causes, which he attempted to analyze. (This notion reflects his experience on the Athenian board of generals and is itself reflected not only in later historical writing, but also in later history, which it influenced by shaping statesmen's understanding of the events with which they had to deal.) A similarly analytical attitude toward human affairs appears in the work of the planner of cities, Hippodamus of Miletus, who remodeled the Piraeus in the 440's and also designed Pericles' Italian colony. He is remembered for his introduction of the gridiron plan for cities, to replace the rabbit warren of winding streets. Hippodamus' work reflected, beside analysis, the experience gained in the centuries of Greek colonization, which had made town planning a recurrent problem. The same experience is reflected in fifth-century architecture, not only in many small refinements —irregularities of line to thwart the effects of perspective, and so on—but also in planning dramatic complexes of public buildings, notably that which crowned the Acropolis, where the Parthenon was made the apex of an area of smaller structures, entered through a monumental gateway.

The same skill in planning human affairs and manipulating men's reactions was applied to the problems of private life, which were more pressing because of the new Athenian way of living. In this new society what should a man attempt and how could he succeed? With the mid-century, professional teachers of "successful living" appeared—men known as "sophists" because they claimed to make one wise (*sophos*). The chief market for their skill was Athens, but they also traveled from city to city, lecturing with great success. Their teaching covered a wide variety of subjects, but especially concerned the art of public speaking. In Athenian democracy political success depended largely on a man's skill as a speaker. And beside politics there was the law: Athenians were litigious, and any man might find himself compelled to argue for his fortune, if not his life, before a court of several hundred of his fellow citizens. It was necessary to speak for oneself, though a writer might be hired to prepare the speech. By their studies of rhetoric, argument (whence logic), and grammar, the sophists laid the basis of Greek higher education, from which was to come the mediaeval university program. By their immediate teaching, however, they—intentionally or unintentionally—obscured the traditional patterns of Greek morality and raised up a generation of skeptics prepared to argue for any action which seemed to their own interest.

In this way the sophists made conspicuous two developments which sprang from causes more general than their teaching. As Athens extended its trading connections and its people became more familiar with the varieties of human behavior, the rightness of its old ways inevitably came to be questioned. Similarly, as the economic and political structure developed, the temptations of power politics and private wealth broke down the old pattern of family and civic discipline. Supervening on this situation, in the year after Pericles' famous speech, the plague of 430 brought the city to the verge of moral chaos. Thucydides, who lived through it, tells how respect for both divine and human law was destroyed by the sudden changes of fortune which made rich men corpses and poor men rich, by the sight of good and bad men dying alike, and by the expectation of death, which destroyed the fear of punishment and the hope of profit, "since men thought their money and their bodies alike to be things of a day." This, though Thucydides could not foresee it, was to be the goal of much Greek philosophy.

At present, however, it was the starting point. For the moral breakdown was both cause and consequence of the rational build-up (of which the argumentative side of sophistry was an example). Once the new habit of coherent, argumentative thought had been turned to moral problems, these problems emerged with a clarity which compelled their discussion and called forth their consequences.

The discussion is obvious: Aristophanes is constantly concerned with such problems; they are the central theme of Thucydides and Herodotus. In philosophy, the Ionian school went out of fashion at Athens; after the plague— and perhaps because of it—the scene was dominated by

Socrates, who turned from cosmology to moral questions. But above all, these questions are the heart of Athenian tragedy.

The basis of the tragedies, as of the works of Aristophanes, Herodotus and Thucydides, is traditional Greek morality, the code which had emerged from the dark ages. Like many codes of primitive societies, this put great emphasis on the maintenance of the established order, the proper subordination of the individual to the human and cosmic society. On the entrance to the temple of Delphi, whose god was the prophet of this old order, were inscribed the precepts, "Nothing too much," and "Know yourself," which meant, "Know your place and stay in it." This was obviously a protection of privilege, but it was also a bill of rights. When a strong man rode roughshod over the weak or a city pressed an advantage too far and destroyed another without mercy or provocation, the victim suffered not only cruelty but also humiliation, the offender was guilty not only of cruelty but also of arrogance, of forgetting his own human nature, his own liability to suffer similar misfortunes. Common humanity was thought to require observance of common decency toward inferiors, if not for the inferiors' sake, then for one's own; there was thought to be some supernatural power which resented arrogance and would surely punish it. Therefore to avoid arrogance was the teaching of common sense, and it is this teaching which fifth-century tragedy and comedy and history reiterate in ever new apologies for the old faith.

But these apologies were not universally convincing. Arrogance sometimes goes unpunished, and there is no clear evidence for its punishment by any supernatural power. Observation established these facts and common sense, especially as represented by the sophists, drew the practical conclusions. Accordingly, Greek society was left without adequate sanction for its moral code and the breakdown became apparent in relations between cities, in city politics, and in the relation of the individual to the city.

Relations between cities were based on the fact that the city was the final object of political loyalty. This was a datum of the traditional morality: no good citizen would sacrifice his city for any other political entity. If the cities would observe common (that is to say, ideal) decency in their relations with each other, all might be well. But when Athens had the opportunity of developing an empire by subjection of her allies, her citizens were not deterred either by the charge of arrogance or the fear of punishment. When the city did fall, Thucydides made its crime and punishment the theme of his acute historical sermon; Herodotus had used the arrogance and defeat of Persia in the same way. But their work did not deter other powers from similar injustices. Greek politics remained a chaos of warring cities in a warfare of which the humane restraints progressively diminished.

Within the city the same loss of restraint shaped the conflict between the classes. This conflict had been sufficiently violent in the time of the tyrants. Now the development of observation and the systematic habit of thought made clear its details and worked out its consequences. Several sophists maintained that the laws of the city represented merely the interests of the rulers, and an unknown writer has left a detailed account of the legal ways by which the common people of Athens protected themselves against their natural enemies, the upper class. Understanding of the economic bases and legal methods of the conflict

made it more severe. This, too, was the effect of its continuance, as Thucydides remarked. Each side was apt to be
embittered by the hostile actions of the other and to re-
taliate yet more savagely. Matters could go so far that
moderates would be distrusted, despised, and killed off by
both sides, and reconciliation could become almost impossible, since neither side would trust the other. In such circumstances even communication almost ceased as words lost
their common meanings and became technical terms for
party demands or pretenses. The only cure was extermina-
tion of one side or the other, or mutual exhaustion. Fortu-
nately, some cities escaped these extremes. In Athens, for
instance, the development of trade provided opportunities
for investment abroad, saved the small farmers from being
bought out, and so preserved a middle group between rich
and poor, which prevented either party from going too far.
Yet even Athens, after her defeat, was to have a reign of
terror under an oligarchy, and many cities were less fortunate than Athens. None wholly escaped the plague of class
conflict; some had less, others more severe, cases; many
suffered repeated attacks. For centuries it remained endemic
in Greece and increased in general frequency and severity.

Thus the discovery that the traditional sanction of the
moral order was false was followed by the gradual breakdown of city life. But the uniform pattern of city life had
provided the standards of individual moral behavior. Those
standards had already been weakened by the influence of
alien ways and of critical thought, by the increase of wealth
and of opportunities for privacy and individualism. The
frequency of exiles in Greek society and the increasing
role of resident aliens in trade were contributing causes
to the same effect. Isolated individuals, whether isolated in

a foreign city or in their own, appear in the literature as dramatic examples of adherence to a moral law which over-rules the discredited, partisan statutes of the city. Sophocles' *Antigone* is the classic literary example: Antigone buried her brother in defiance of a city ordinance prohibiting the action on pain of death; she was apprehended and put to death; and the gods manifested their displeasure by punishing the ruler of the city.

In the *Antigone* the moral law is represented as the law of Zeus. But while men were losing belief in the general divine power which maintained the moral order, belief in the particular Olympian gods could not survive. The particular gods had been composite beings, anyhow—essentially powers acting in nature, superficially persons described by Homer and Hesiod. Systematic thought about them now rejected the poetic descriptions. This undermined the customary rituals—one prays and brings gifts to a person, not to a cosmic power—but it did not produce an acceptable theology. The damage to the rituals was not immediately apparent: they were perpetuated by law, custom, and superstition, so as to be somewhat independent of their supposed significance. But the failure to produce an acceptable theology was at once and acutely felt. Already in Aeschylus' *Prometheus Bound* a myth of conflict between the gods was made the dramatic representation of the conflict between rule and compassion. Prometheus, an immortal being, pitied men and stole fire from heaven for them. Thus he thwarted Zeus's plan to let them perish, and Zeus punished him by crucifying him on a peak in the Caucasus. But he knew a secret which Zeus must learn if his rule was to endure. Zeus demanded it; Prometheus refused to tell; Zeus resorted to further tortures. In sum:

the requirements of rule are tyrannical, the impulses of compassion, anarchic. We may see the resultant tragedy in the history of Aeschylus' time, for example, in Athens' subjection of the Delian league, but the poet saw it as a conflict in nature itself, from which both the physical world and human history emerge. If such conflicts rage in nature, there can be no confident appeal from the law of the state to "the law of Zeus." This was certainly not the conclusion Aeschylus would have drawn; he wrote a second play to explain the reconciliation of his conflicting principles. But it was the first play which expressed the thought and commanded the attention of the next generation. The second play was lost.

Euripides devoted a series of plays to conflicts between the human sense of justice and the legends of the gods. Greatest of these plays is *The Bacchae*, which deals with the coming of Dionysus to Thebes. Dionysus' power made the women of the city leave their homes to range the hills as *bacchae* (manic worshipers of the god). When the ruler of the city attempted to maintain order, the god deprived him of his reason, made him ridiculous, and led him out to the hills, where he was caught and torn to pieces by a troop of the manic women headed by his mother. The terror of the play comes from the poet's sympathy with both sides. The god is undeniably a god, a source of supernatural power and joy, but his power destroys the good order of the city, makes folly of the common sense of prudent men, and blinds its victims to the deepest attachments of ordinary life. The fact that it is irresistible makes it all the more unjust. Thus the appeal from the law of the city to the law of the god is reduced to a mere appeal from the will of one ruler to that of another; it loses any pretense to justice.

But if divine and civil law alike represent no more than the wills of rulers, where can justice be found? The question was raised in deadly earnest by the most important example in history of an individual's defiance of his society —the trial of Socrates in 399.

Socrates was a stone carver; his concern for philosophy was an example of the extension of cultural interests in Athens to the middle class. In his early years he studied the cosmological theories of the Ionians. He made a name for himself; the oracle at Delphi is said to have declared him the wisest of men. Perhaps by this, perhaps by the success of the sophists, he was turned to the problem of wisdom and dropped cosmology. To investigate the nature of wisdom he made a practice of cross-questioning, in public, men thought to be wise. This got him a host of enemies and a circle of devoted followers, especially young men. His followers imitated his methods, to the intense irritation of their interrogated elders. The teaching of a method of argument, the destructive questioning of accepted moral and theological beliefs, the concern with wisdom and the reputation of his earlier cosmological studies combined to connect him in public opinion with the sophists. He was anxious to avoid the connection and appealed especially to the social, rather than philosophical, distinction, that he never taught for pay. But the evidence was not clear. The sophists taught the rich who could pay their fees, and many of their arguments favored their patrons. Socrates' following included rich young men, and a number of these went on to attack democracy. Socrates himself had probably questioned the presuppositions of democratic government, as of the other forms of Athenian behavior. To what extent he went beyond questioning to positive teaching is uncertain. Since half a dozen of his followers later taught half a dozen different kinds of philosophy, it seems likely that his teaching was chiefly limited to example, not only of the method of questioning, but also of the philosophic life, the life contemptuous of possessions and bodily comforts "as things of a day" and devoted entirely to the investigation of intellectual questions. Popular suspicion probably attributed to him specific doctrines. He was finally brought to trial on the charge of corrupting the youth and not believing in the gods which the city believed in but in other new supernatural powers. He was found guilty.

Then, if we can believe Plato's story of the trial, came the essential question. Since the offense had no fixed penalty, the prosecutor and the condemned had each to propose penalties and the court to choose between them. The prosecutor proposed death. Socrates proposed that he be given free meals at public expense for the rest of his life (a common civic honor). His friends persuaded him to change his proposal to a fine, but this did not save him and should not obscure the significance of his original proposal. The individual had flatly refused to accept the authority of the city. The city, through its official, incorrupt tribunal, by democratic procedure, had found his actions criminal and deserving punishment. He admitted the actions, but refused to accept the judgment, and Plato reports that he declared he would continue the actions. The authority in question of right and wrong, therefore, was not the civil court, but his own conscience. That he subsequently refused to escape from jail and therefore voluntarily submitted to the death penalty is immaterial; the question was not of compliance with the punishment, but of acceptance of the court's finding as correct. Socrates had tried Athens for impiety and had condemned it.

CHAPTER IV

Disintegration

THE fall of Athens in 404 ended the possibility of any Greek city's creating an empire which would unite the Mediterranean basin. Sparta was now the greatest power in Greece. She had claimed to be fighting Athens in order to liberate the Greek cities; she now liberated them by installing oligarchic governments—under the protection of Spartan overseers and garrisons. The Spartans made up for their lack of money at home by venality and extortion abroad, while the oligarchs revenged themselves on their opponents and filled the cities with bloodshed. In Athens there was a reign of terror under the "thirty tyrants," headed by one Critias, a former follower of Socrates (his role at this time did much to secure his teacher's condemnation five years later). Since Sparta did not have the strength to maintain all these governments against the local oppositions they aroused, revolutions took place, and her control outside the Peloponnese began to disintegrate. Then, in 401 she lost the support of Persia.

Persian support had originally been given her on the agreement that when Athens should be defeated the Greek cities of Asia Minor would be returned to Persian control.

This agreement had been honored. But the Persian Viceroy in Asia Minor, Cyrus "the Younger," had been friendly to the Greeks, not only because of his admiration for Greek culture (and his Ionian mistress), but also because he wanted Greek support for an attempt to overthrow his elder brother, the Great King. He encouraged the Greek coastal cities to revolt from their satraps and put themselves under his protection. Sparta contributed seven hundred hoplites to his army; beside these he was able to raise over twelve thousand Greek troops, mostly mercenaries. With these and his oriental forces he marched into Babylonia and was killed in battle. (His Greek troops refused to surrender and marched up the Tigris and across Armenia to the Black Sea; of the 13,000, 8,600 survived, among them Xenophon, another follower of Socrates, whose account of the expedition in his *Anabasis* is a masterpiece of war reporting.) After Cyrus' death the Persian authorities in Asia Minor tried to reconquer the Greek cities and these appealed to Sparta. Sparta, which had been alienated from the Great King by her support of Cyrus, now saw the opportunity to acquire an empire. This involved a war in Asia Minor, where her commanders distinguished themselves in looting, but failed to build any stable domain.

Persia retaliated by financing the resistance to Sparta in Greece, and soon had Sparta involved in war with Thebes, Athens, and Corinth. Things went so badly for the Spartans that they had to recall most of their forces from Asia Minor in 394, and in that same year a Persian fleet under an Athenian admiral destroyed the Spartan fleet. This encouraged many coastal and island cities to drive out their Spartan overseers. Next the long walls of Athens, which had been destroyed in 404, were rebuilt with Persian help in 393, and the city was strengthened by the return of some of its colonies.

Athens no sooner began to regain its power than it tried to rebuild its alliances with the Ionian cities and re-establish its control over the entrance to the Black Sea. Also it supported a Greek Cypriote king named Evagoras, who had revolted against the Persians. This determined the Persians to help Sparta against Athens. Presently both sides wearied of the war, and in 386 the Great King was able to dictate a peace by which Persia got Cyprus and the mainland cities of Ionia, but the remaining cities of Greece, except for three Athenian colonies, were to be autonomous. Thus the Greek cities got their liberty—as a gift from the Great King and at the price of (1) the abandonment of Ionia and Cyprus, (2) the disintegration of political order in Greece above the city-state level, and (3) the continuance of the Spartan hegemony.

Items (2) and (3) of this bill were implied by autonomy: so long as each city could determine its own policies, no powerful league could be formed. Local antipathies were such everywhere that some states in any area would certainly refuse to join; domestic conflicts were such in many cities that if one party voted to join the other would certainly oppose, and as soon as the local government changed hands the league would lose a member. But so long as no powerful league could be formed, Sparta was expected to remain the dominant power in Greece.

So matters stood for eight years (387–379), during which Sparta violated the peace on several occasions by interfering in the domestic affairs of smaller states. The most conspicuous violation occurred in Thebes, where a Spartan general took the citadel by surprise and installed

a garrison and a government of quislings. In 379 Theban
conspirators arranged an intimate party for the chief officials of the government; when the servants were dismissed
and the women brought in they turned out to be not
women, but Theban patriots in disguise. After the murder
of the officials, the political prisoners were set free and the
garrison forced to surrender. Thereupon Sparta went to
war with Thebes.

Thebes found an ally in Athens, which had spent the past
eight years making alliances with individual Aegean cities
and took this opportunity to transform them into a new
league, made acceptable to the minor allies by constitutional provisions which they thought would prevent the
re-establishment of an Athenian tyranny. They were mis-
taken. Once Athens regained her power she began to
neglect these provisions, and all that saved the minor states
from a renewal of her rule was her final inability to impose
it on them. For the present, however, the affairs of the allies
went well. A naval victory over the Spartans enabled
Athens to renew her connections with western Greece.
The Thebans were even more successful. A body of shock
troops, "the Sacred Band," composed of a hundred and
fifty pairs of lovers, was organized; the Spartans were
repeatedly defeated, and the cities of Boeotia were united
in a league of which Thebes was in control. These Theban
triumphs convinced the Athenians that they might soon
have more to fear from Thebes than from Sparta; accordingly they made a separate peace with the Spartans in 371.

Athens' withdrawal left Sparta free to deal with Thebes.
But a Theban general, Epaminondas, devised a new military formation: instead of a line of uniform depth to
meet the enemy's line, he thinned out the right and center

and massed his best troops, with the Sacred Band in front, on his left wing. With these he could smash the enemy's right, then turn and take their remaining troops on the unprotected side, since shields were worn on the left. He thus defeated the Spartan army which invaded Boeotia in 371, and his victory touched off a series of revolutions in which the pro-Spartan oligarchies of Peloponnesian cities were overthrown. These changes gave the cities of Arcadia courage to form a league for mutual protection against Sparta, and next year Epaminondas invaded the Peloponnese to support them. The territory of Sparta was ravaged; a capital city for the league—Megalopolis—was founded just over the northwest boundary of Sparta; Messenia was liberated and a city, Messene, built to be its center. The Spartan hegemony in Greece was ended forever.

But Epaminondas could no more build a stable political structure than the Spartans could before him. So long as most Greeks would be loyal to nothing larger than their own city-states, the predominance of any one state was a signal for the others to unite against it in defense of their own liberty. No sooner had Thebes established the Arcadian League than the Arcadians began to look for support against Thebes. They found it in Athens. But Athens had already entered the war on the side of Sparta. So by 366 Arcadia was allied both to Athens and to Thebes, which were at war with each other, and Athens both to Arcadia and to Sparta, which were at war with each other. Thebes wasted itself in the fighting engendered by such combinations and lost its hegemony at the death of Epaminondas in 362.

By this time mainland Greece was in such disorder that the insignificant district of Phocis, bordering on Delphi, was able to become a major power in the years after 356 simply by seizing the treasures of the shrine and hiring some ten thousand mercenaries. Border wars flickered off and on for another ten years and finally laid the country open to the intervention of King Philip II of Macedon.

Characteristic of the fourth century was the development of a new kind of state, larger than a city, more civilized and more complex than a tribal kingdom, but smaller than the ancient empires. These new states developed around the periphery of the Greek world and were sometimes ruled by Greeks, sometimes by natives, but were always largely Greek in culture and native in population. They represent the second stage in the hellenization of the western world. The first had been the dissemination of Greek artifacts and customs through trade and colonization. By the fourth century, however, the Greeks had become rulers of the natives or the natives had learned the art of rule from the Greeks. In either event provincial concentrations of power were developed with the new political and economic skill.

In south Russia, at the entrance to the Sea of Azov, the Milesian colony of Panticapaeum became the center of a kingdom which included both Greek cities and native subjects, and prospered not only by export of grain and fish to the Aegean cities but also as middleman for Greek trade with the Scythians of the steppes.

In the southwest corner of Asia Minor the Carians, under their dynast Mausolus, won virtual independence from Persia, conquered a number of Greek cities along the coast, won over several Aegean islands in the 350's, and stopped Athens' attempt to reconstitute her empire in that region. (The tomb of Mausolus and his wife was decorated by outstanding Greek sculptors; its fame lives on in the word "mausoleum.")

In Cyprus, Evagoras, a king of one of the Greek cities, managed with Athenian support to get control of almost the whole island in the 380's. We saw above that this caused Persia to shift her support in Greece from Athens back to Sparta. By the peace of 386 Athens was required to abandon Evagoras, and then the Persians by a long war succeeded in reducing his territory to his original city.

In Sicily, Dionysius I, tyrant of Syracuse, defeated a Carthaginian attempt to conquer the island and almost succeeded in driving the Carthaginians out. When he died in 367 he was ruler of most of Sicily, the toe and heel of Italy, and territories along the coast of the Adriatic. Although his court had been a center of Greek culture, his territories contained a large non-Greek population of Sicilians and Italians, and his rule rested partially on their support, sometimes against the Greeks.

In central Italy Rome had already adopted elements of Greek civilization and was gradually conquering its neighbors and uniting them to itself.

In northern Greece, finally, was Macedon, a wild country of semi-Greek population ruled in Homeric fashion by kings who had acquired a non-Homeric taste for the culture of the city-states. They imported Greek artists, writers, and scholars to ornament their court and took advantage of Greek economic, military, and technical innovations to strengthen themselves against their vassal chieftains.

Philip II, King of the Macedonians, followed this policy with particular success. As a youth he had been a hostage in Thebes and had observed Epaminondas. When the army gave him the Macedonian crown in 359 he immediately set about remodeling the army. To Epaminondas' use of heavy formations led by a corps of shock troops, now "the Foot Companions" of the King, he added a larger role for his cavalry, "the Companions." After testing his work by the subjugation of his inland vassals, he attacked Amphipolis: the gold mines were essential for his ambitions. Amphipolis appealed to Athens, but Philip made a treaty with Athens by which he undertook to conquer Amphipolis and give it to Athens in return for Pydna. He took Amphipolis in 357, Pydna in 356, and kept both. Athens was busy with the revolt of the eastern Aegean islands, instigated by Mausolus of Caria, and did nothing. By the time she had lost her war (355), Philip was preparing for further advances: three years later he took Thessaly, next he subjugated Thrace, next he took Chalcidice, city by city, in 350–348. Athens sent help to the Chalcidian cities, but too little and too late. Philip paused to organize his conquests and resubjugate Thrace. Then in 346 he made peace with Athens and immediately struck at central Greece, crushed Phocis, got control of Delphi, proclaimed a general peace, and began preparations for war against the Illyrians. It took him three years to secure his western and northwestern frontiers and reorganize Thessaly, then he was ready to annex Thrace completely and conquer the Greek cities along the entrance to the Black Sea, especially Byzantium. The Black Sea was Athens' granary, and she had colonies and allies among the cities along the entrance. Therefore, when Philip attacked Byzantium in 340, she declared war and sent her forces to protect Byzantium, but took no effective steps to protect herself. Before she knew it Philip had passed Thermopylae. She allied with Thebes and a number of minor states in a last-minute attempt to stop him. The allies were defeated at Chaironea in 338; a campaign in the Peloponnese completed the subjugation of Greece, Macedonian garrisons were established in Thebes, Corinth, and Chalcis, and the Greek cities were organized in a league under Macedonian control. Philip proclaimed a general peace and put the league to work in preparation for war against Persia. In 336 he was assassinated by a man of no position, reportedly because he had refused to right a wrong done by one of his generals.

The political disintegration of Greece in the fourth century was accompanied by economic decline. The constant wars devastated the countryside; travel and trade were interrupted, crops and buildings burned, trees and vines cut down, wells filled in. Not a few cities were captured and looted, some were destroyed. For the remaining cities, even worse than war were the consequences of the continuing social conflict, sharpened by the increase of poverty and the frequent changes of the political situation. Every decisive battle was followed by revolutions deposing the governments which had depended on the support of the defeated power. Every revolution meant fighting, destruction, a legacy of hatred within the city and interruption of its trade abroad.

Overseas trade was also diminished by the wars, by the growth of piracy, resulting from the lack of any strong naval power to police the seas, and especially by the disturbed conditions in countries which had been among the principal markets of Greece. Asia Minor and the Phoenician coasts were torn by repeated rebellions of satraps. Egypt broke away from Persia at the beginning of the century and was chronically at war until reconquered in 343. In

Sicily the Carthaginian invasions and the wars of Dionysius I at the beginning of the century destroyed almost all the Greek cities except Syracuse; what rebuilding Dionysius did was largely destroyed in the long civil wars which broke out in 357, ten years after his death. The Greek cities of south Italy suffered much from Dionysius, but more from the pressure of Italian tribes; they had to appeal repeatedly for help from Greece.

But even with areas not seriously damaged by war, Greek trade declined, because of the spread of hellenization: local manufacturers now turned out imitations of Greek wares which undersold the genuine articles. The vine and olive had been transplanted to the colonies and colonial wine and oil diminished the demand for the Greek products.

The decline of foreign trade, together with the destruction of property and interruption of production at home, caused a depression in Greece which lasted from the fall of Athens to the Macedonian conquest. The sufferings occasioned by this depression were made more severe by the consequences of overpopulation.

One thing war did not make scarce was people. (Greek wars were not usually very destructive of life: the victims had to be chased on foot and killed by hand, and it was more economical to sell them.) Therefore the fourth century saw an increase in the practice of abandoning newborn children, especially girls. Nevertheless, the population declined only slowly. In 336 the population of Athens was still perhaps one half of what it had been at its peak in 431. For Athens without her empire this was too much. Overpopulation and depression together caused a constant shortage of food, sometimes approaching famine for several years on end. Athenian legislation regulating the grain trade was accordingly severe: transactions which made profiteering possible were punishable by death.

In these circumstances the Greek city was forced further toward the welfare state. The political strength of the urban poor was increased as they were joined in the city by the small farmers whose lands had been devastated by the incessant wars. This required an extension of public services, especially the maintenance of gymnasia and public doctors. Moreover, the unemployed had to be fed. Their need exacerbated the social conflicts of which we have already seen the pattern established in the fifth century. That Athens got through the fourth century without direct and violent class warfare shows not only her citizens' loyalty to the democratic tradition and abomination for the memory of the "thirty tyrants," but also their success in maintaining their trading connections even when their empire was lost. Besides trade, Athens profited greatly from the development of commercial banking, which advanced rapidly in this century and of which she was the center. Income from trade and banking may be supposed to have been important among the factors which enabled her to introduce pay for all citizens who attended the assembly. Pay for service in the court continued as usual. Besides this, any surplus revenue was used for the fund to pay for attendance at the theaters. The board which managed this fund became the most influential body in the state, and the most important political consideration was to keep the payments high. This limited the amounts available for military expenditure and made impossible the reconstitution of the Athenian empire and effective resistance to Macedon.

But the welfare state provided only a minimum. Between

those who wanted more, competition was intense. Once again great numbers of Greeks began to go abroad to make their fortunes, but now they rarely went as colonies, usually as individuals hoping to find employment. Greek artists, doctors, and men of science entered the service of the Great King and his satraps and of the Pharaoh of Egypt; Greek merchants and prostitutes settled in their cities; Greek soldiers served as mercenaries in their armies. The ten thousand who marched with Cyrus the Younger were only the most famous. Greek mercenaries often formed the bodyguards of the satraps; they were among the chief supports of the independent government of Egypt; when the satraps revolted or the Great King attempted to reconquer Egypt they were employed by the tens of thousands on both sides.

On men who remained in Greece, competition imposed specialization. As remarked in the military history, specially trained bands of soldiers were organized and played important roles, notably the Sacred Band at Thebes and the Companions of the Macedonian kings. Even more important was the role of mercenaries who became specialists in the art of fighting (and the art of getting paid for fighting without actually doing it). Such men were the products of the depression and the century's constant revolutions and exilings. Their influence and numbers reached a peak in the early fifties during the hegemony of Phocis, which rested almost entirely upon them. But they were a major factor in most of the armies of the century, especially the Athenian. The citizen army was ever less able to meet such professional competition, and men were less willing to serve in it as individualism increased and loyalty to the city-state declined.

With the professional army went the professional general, the expert not to be matched by an amateur serving for a year, nor by a politician who had been general for years on end but was unfamiliar with battles. Similarly, the development of advanced banking methods made a career in finance a matter for specialization. And the development of rhetoric and its practice in Athens produced another specialist, the political public speaker. The sophists had taught and practiced public speaking, but had not usually meddled directly with politics, though they had discussed general questions of political theory. Their type did not disappear; its greatest representative in the fourth century was Isocrates of Athens, a professional speech-writer and teacher of speaking, whose school drew students from all parts of the Greek world but whose political activity did not go much beyond advocacy of a pan-hellenic union for an attack on Persia—a dream he saw realized, just before his death, by Philip II of ·Macedon. In contrast to Isocrates were the political orators of his time, especially Demosthenes, who was constantly urging the people of Athens to take particular actions to stop the advance of Philip. Thus the leadership of the state came to be divided between three groups of specialists: the generals (mostly abroad and out of touch with the people), the financial officials, and the political orators. From time to time the generals had to suspend operations for want of public support, the financiers vetoed necessary actions abroad and spent money at home on military installations which proved useless, and the orators moved the people to adopt policies which they had neither the military strength nor the money to carry out.

Similar specialization appears during the fourth century

in most aspects of Greek life and usually with the same consequences—increased technical skill and diminished understanding of the ramifications of what is done. It is clear, for instance, in the arts and crafts, and especially in the sculpture of Praxiteles, the greatest artist of the age and (to judge from the number of preserved imitations of his works) the most influential artist of antiquity. Earlier sculpture had usually been related to its architectural setting, now the emphasis was on the individual statue. The social setting also was neglected: hitherto cult statues had represented the gods as attending to the worshiper and concerned about his worship, but the gods of Praxiteles were often represented as completely unaware of the onlooker. This has been variously explained. It has been said that they were not intended to be cult statues (objects of worship), but merely votive statues. It has been said that they reflected the new, Epicurean notion of the gods as living in bliss, indifferent to the world of men. It has been said that the artist was indifferent to the religious functions for which his statues might be used and was concerned merely to produce representations of beautiful human bodies, caught in moments of languid movement or repose. The exquisite young man, with one hip thrust out, lounging against a tree trunk, was called Hermes or Apollo or Dionysus; the woman, magnificent in her nakedness, was Aphrodite. These statues, like the orations of Demosthenes, are perfect compositions, calculated to win the admiration of the audience, but they underrate the power they pretend to describe.

Praxiteles' choice of gods was significant: Aphrodite and her son, Eros, the young god of love, Apollo as god of poetic inspiration, Dionysus as patron of drunkenness, re-

ligious ecstasy, and the hope of individual immortality—
these had become the gods of private life and of the individual. As loyalty to the city-state declined, so did the
representation of the civic deities and so did their worship
(except as prescribed by law and carried out by civic
officials as part of their duties). Specialists now appear in
the divine realm as well as the human. One of the most
successful was Asclepius who specialized in healing. His
worshipers were many and sincere.

As the gods specialized, so did the philosophers. Socrates
had combined, with dialectic, common sense and concern
about moral problems, with indifference to hardship and
public opinion, the life of a man about town. His followers took the various sides of this personality by themselves
and pushed them to extremes. A school in Megara developed his dialectic to serve an implausible metaphysics
drawn from Parmenides. Xenophon saw in him the paragon
of common sense and the virtues of the old fashioned
gentleman. Antisthenes saw in him the paragon of virtue,
but thought that his virtue was manifested by his indifference to hardship and public opinion. Since these are apt
to be undermined by concern for pleasure, pleasure is evil.
Since pleasure is evil and hardship and ill-repute are matters
of indifference, the virtuous man is self-sufficient. Antisthenes, who was poor, paraded his self-sufficiency and
his torn clothes. (His teaching lived on to influence Diogenes, who in the 350's developed the notion that man to
be happy need only train himself to have as few needs as
possible and satisfy them directly and shamelessly. Accordingly, he lived like an animal, was nicknamed "dog"—
kyon—and gave his name to the Cynic school which derived from his teachings.) At the opposite extreme from

Antisthenes was Aristippus of Cyrene, another of Socrates' pupils. Like Xenophon he started from Socrates' common sense, but with this he combined Socrates' enjoyment of the pleasures of life about town. This led him to declare happiness the goal of life and pleasure the occasion of happiness. Accordingly he made a fortune as a fashionable sophist and favorite of tyrants. Around these men and their differences grew up a literature of apocryphal anecdotes which testify to the popular interest that seized and oversimplified their teachings: Aristippus going to dinner passed Diogenes washing garlic in a gutter. He said to him, "Poor Diogenes, if you knew how to get on with people you wouldn't have to live like that." "Poor Aristippus," said Diogenes, "if you knew how to live like this you wouldn't have to get on with people."

Above these sectarian followers of Socrates, above the disintegration of the fourth century, above its trivial and tragic history, towers Plato. His work united the various facets of Socratic teaching—argumentation, common sense, concern for the Greek tradition, moral concern, asceticism, and delight in good company, especially that of beautiful young men. To these he added from his own genius the sensitivity of a poet, a literary style of amazing adaptability and power, and a habit of reflection which never let go of an idea, but elicited every consequence, so that a simple question might lead to the most complex problems of metaphysics. Finally, he had been shaped by the history of his city. Born in 429, his youth and young manhood had coincided with the disasters of the Second Peloponnesian War and the terror following. (Critias, the worst of the "thirty tyrants" had been one of his relatives.) In the tragic stupidities of Athens he had found one man whose clear intelligence had revealed to him the joy of understanding and the beauty of the relationships of the propositions in an argument, a beauty of which music and even mathematics seemed to him mere images. This man had been Socrates. Athenian democracy had condemned him to death in 399, when Plato was thirty. Plato thereupon had left the city for twelve years of travel (he was rich).

From these experiences—and perhaps from his aristocratic family—came his contempt and distrust of the common man. Therefore when he finally came back to the city and started to teach, he did not talk to anybody he met in the street, as Socrates had. Instead he chose a spot near a gymnasium in a pleasant suburb called Academia and established there a select society for the worship of the Muses, the goddesses of music, poetry and the dance. There, except for two short visits to Sicily, he remained until his death in 347. Members of the society went on teaching there until the Christian emperor Justinian suppressed the school in A.D. 529. Such formation of a new center of loyalty, a private religious association apart from the cult of the city, was common at the time, especially for the worship of foreign divinities brought to Athens by trade. But Plato used the common form (and its privileges) for his peculiar purposes.

One purpose of the Academy—as the association and its property came to be called—was to enable Plato to keep his teaching secret. There were some essential points on which he did not think it wise to commit his thoughts to writing. Therefore it is not possible to reconstruct with certainty what he taught in the Academy. But it is by his written works, not by his teaching in the Academy, that he has influenced all subsequent western philosophical and theological thought. In that influence three major elements are clear:

First there is the method of question and answer, which analyzes every discussion to a structure of specific points, each of which must be established or attacked by definite arguments. This leads both to study of the forms of argument and to systematic treatment of philosophic problems, tendencies of which the consequences will be apparent in Plato's pupil, Aristotle. It also plays a large part in rationalistic criticism of established forms of behavior and common notions of the gods, the destructive side of Plato's thought, which contributed much to the formation of the hellenistic temper and, later, of Jewish and Christian attacks on paganism.

Second there is the dualism. For Plato there were two worlds, one of physical objects in constant change, the other of unchanging forms. Change and the changeless were united in every physical object: a river was unchangingly a river because of its form, yet was constantly changing, so that no precise statement as to its volume or shape could ever be true long enough to be made. You could know exactly what "a river" was, because you knew the form; you could never know exactly one particular river, because it did not cease changing while you learned it. Since what is known must be, the world of forms, the knowable world, was also the world of being, the world of the mind, the world of light and beauty, the concern of the philosopher. But the world of physical objects was the world of change, therefore of ignorance and darkness, the world of the body, the concern of the vulgar craftsman. Therefore the philosopher was to train himself to neglect the body and look at the true beauty of forms and their relationships. Since physical pleasures concentrate our attention on bodies and make us concerned about them, the philosopher was to avoid such pleasures; his life was to be devoted to disengaging himself from the body, to developing his awareness of forms. Here the asceticism already seen in Sparta and in Socrates was justified by a metaphysical system which created an "other world" of eternal forms, quite different from the "other world" of the gods on Mount Olympus. Plato tried to fuse these two realms of better beings, and subsequent attempts appear in such theologies as make some deity at once a form and a person —at once *something*, like Being or Truth or Love, and *Somebody*, who is and speaks and loves.

Third there is the literary art and the poetry: much Greek philosophical writing shows influence by Plato's style, notably by his vocabulary and his metaphors, for instance, his description of philosophy as initiation into a mystery. Of his literary devices the dialogue was often used, but even more important were the myths to which he resorted when he would not or could not state his beliefs clearly. In these myths Plato the poet was free to speak. He spoke especially of the immortality of the soul and often drew on Orphic fantasies about an afterlife of rewards and punishments. The incorporation of such material in the works of Plato gave it a prestige and perpetuity it otherwise would never have enjoyed. Akin to the myths are the imaginative creations, notably the ideal state described in the Republic and the figure of Socrates. The ideal state turned out to be a modified Sparta ruled by an idealized Plato. It has been a source of inspiration for political reformers, especially totalitarians, even since. Perhaps Plato's most pernicious contribution to western civilization was the notion that true freedom is freedom to do what you ought; this enables advocates of almost any restraints to claim they are defending the "true" freedom of their victims. The figure of Socrates created by Plato was basically the real Socrates, but made to teach Platonic metaphysics and perhaps chastened to accord with its teaching. It exercised a wide influence as a moral example, especially through the dialogues dealing with Socrates' trial, imprisonment, and death, which began the formation of the figure of the martyr, important in Christianity and Judaism.

By the many sides of his genius, Plato stood apart from the specialists characteristic of the fourth century. Yet in his works he continually pleaded for specialization. Dialogue after dialogue contains the argument: if you wanted to know about some physical object you would consult an expert, therefore in moral and philosophical questions you should also consult an expert—a philosopher. But the philosopher, although a specialist, was not yet a professional—Socrates had attempted to separate himself from the sophists by insisting on his amateur standing; Plato's private fortune enabled him to follow this tradition.

Plato's pupil Aristotle became the outstanding example of the professional philosopher, and his most important achievement was to lay the basis for what may be called the general theory of specialization. The existence of specialists raises the problem of the relationship of their specialties. The solution to this problem must be a systematic account of all knowledge, an account which leaves the details of the particular fields to specialists, but describes the essential content of each field and its place in the general structure of what is known. In this way the intellectual and cultural disintegration of the fourth cen-

tury led to a new and larger synthesis, as the political disintegration led to a new and larger political unit. But in
the intellectual field the progress was slow. Aristotle did
not produce the synthesis needed, but he prepared for it
by his classification of the ways in which objects can differ
(hence, the categories of knowledge), by his study of the
nature of definition and of proof, by his detailed accounts
of a number of fields of knowledge (logic, metaphysics,
physics, zoology, psychology, ethics, political theory, rhetoric), and by his creation of much scientific terminology.
His works show the technical development characteristic
of the age; it was doubtless their technicality which limited
their influence. As times grew more troubled, men needed
direct and simple solutions to the problems of life. Therefore the influence of Aristotle's works was felt chiefly
within a small circle of his students who established a
school in the legal form of a corporation for the worship
of the Muses, on the model of Plato's Academy. The
Aristotelian school, which came to be called the Lyceum,
led a rather obscure existence. Not until the Middle Ages
were Aristotle's classifications to become the blueprints
of the structure of learning.

CHAPTER V

Dissemination ⌇⌇⌇⌇⌇⌇⌇⌇⌇⌇

PHILIP'S assassination in 336 brought Macedon to the verge of collapse. Her subjects in the south and east were ready to revolt, her enemies in the north and west to attack; Persia had been alienated by the preparations for invasion; and at home the royal family was split by the rivalry of Philip's wives. But Philip's son Alexander had already shown outstanding ability. Important generals now gave him their support, the other likely claimants to the throne were liquidated, and the young King (just turned twenty) was able to act promptly against the revolt in Greece.

From then on he continued acting with amazing promptitude against one enemy after another, until his death in 323. In these thirteen years he conquered Greece, Illyria, Thrace, the west coast and center of Asia Minor, the Phoenician coast, Egypt, Mesopotamia, Babylonia, Persia, the eastern reaches of the Persian empire, and beyond. At his death his rule extended from the first cataract of the Nile to the upper reaches of the Jaxartes in central Asia, and from the eastern affluents of the Indus to the Adriatic. In the course of his career he had overthrown the Persian empire and put its vast treasure back into circulation; he

had destroyed Thebes, Tyre, and a number of minor cities
and had founded eighteen or twenty Alexandrias. In these
and other settlements and garrisons he had established tens
of thousands of Macedonians and Greeks in military control of the areas conquered. Along with them he had maintained many of the native civil administrators. He had created an army in which Macedonian, Greek, and oriental
forces were combined; he was moving toward the creation
of a kingdom in which they would be combined. This
kingdom would have as its center not a people, but a man.
Loyalty to the King already bound together the Macedonians; he hoped it would transcend both the loyalties of
the Greeks to their declining city-states and the tribal
and local loyalties of his eastern subjects. To make himself
such an object of loyalty he had become in Persia the
Great King, in Egypt the divine Pharaoh, son of the god
Amon, and in Greece, by official action of the Greek
cities, on his own demand, a god.

The deity's untimely demise in 323 defeated his plans,
but did not destroy their influence. The men around him
had caught something of his complex thought and appropriated different aspects of it. Some were loyal to his
memory and tried to keep his empire intact for his post-
humous son; others tried to keep the empire intact, but
to usurp control of it; yet others set up local kingdoms of
their own in the territories they were appointed to govern.
In the ensuing wars the would-be usurpers and local
dynasts combined to defeat the loyalists, and Alexander's
family was exterminated by about 310. Next the local
dynasts combined against the would-be usurpers and defeated them. Matters were complicated by a barbarian
invasion. In 279 the Galatians (Celts) overran Macedonia,

raided Greece as far as Delphi, and returned to ravage
Thrace, whence some of them crossed into Asia Minor and
eventually settled in the center of the peninsula. Their
withdrawal from Greece and Macedonia was followed by
local wars for the control of those countries, and it was not
until 276, almost half a century after Alexander's death, that
the main outlines of the division of his empire were finally
settled. By that time: (1) India had been lost to a native
dynasty. (2) In Egypt a general named Ptolemy had established himself on Alexander's model as King and Pharaoh;
as King he had ruled (besides Egypt) Libya, Palestine,
Cyprus, and cities along the coasts of Phoenicia and Asia
Minor and in the Aegean islands. He had died in 283 and
had been succeeded by his son, Ptolemy II. (3) In Macedonia, Antigonus II, the grandson of a general of the same
name, now succeeded to Alexander's original position as
King of the Macedonians. He and his dynasty were to
continue the attempt to subject the cities of Greece and
the Aegean to Macdeonian control. (4) The bulk of the
former Persian empire—most of Asia Minor, Syria, Mesopotamia, Babylonia, Persia, and points east to the mountains bordering the Indus and the upper reaches of the
Jaxartes—had been acquired by a general named Seleucus,
who had thus succeeded to Alexander's claims as Great
King. Northeastern Asia Minor had never been conquered,
and after Seleucus' death in 280 his son Antiochus had lost
the center of the country to the Galatians and consequently
had difficulty in holding the western coast.

Besides the three large kingdoms which had arisen from
Alexander's empire, the life of the Greek cities in Greece
and the hellenization of the Black Sea region and the western Mediterranean went on as before.

Within the Greek cities the social conflict continued to produce factions and revolutions, while externally the cities went on fighting with each other and at the same time tried to fight off Macedon. Since the Macedonians concentrated on the major cities, especially Corinth and Athens, the minor ones now formed leagues which carried on the resistance. Most important were the Aetolian League in central Greece just north of the Gulf of Corinth and the Achaean League along the north shore of the Peloponnese. These leagues contained no cities large enough to dominate them as Athens and Thebes had dominated the Delian and Boeotian leagues; therefore they afforded more successful examples of federal government, but the development was fortuitous, indicated no real change in Greek loyalties, and came too late. (The same must be said of the increased resort to arbitration in disputes between cities and of the attempt to palliate civil conflicts by submitting law suits to judges imported from other towns.)

In the basin of the Black Sea, Panticapaeum continued its pre-eminence on the northern coast; on the southern coast the native but hellenized kingdoms of Bithynia and Pontus became important as inland rivals to the Greek cities of the shore. They had protected themselves from the Seleucids by inviting the Galatians to invade Asia Minor, and the Galatian country now lay between them and the Seleucid power.

In Sicily renewed civil wars had led to the development of a new Syracusan tyranny under an adventurer named Agathocles, who at one time had invaded North Africa, at another time, controlled southern Italy and reached across the Adriatic to seize Corcyra. His power had collapsed with his death in 289, after which the pressure of the Italians on the Greek cities had led them to call for help from Greece. The latest leader to answer the call had been Pyrrhus, King of Epirus, and by 276 Pyrrhus had defeated the Romans in a series of battles which cost him so many men that the term "Pyrrhic victory" became proverbial. He had also defeated the Carthaginians in Sicily, and his victories had so frightened his Greek allies that they were already intriguing against him. This withdrawal of Greek support, the dwindling of his own forces, and the chance of taking Macedon from its new possessor, Antigonus II, determined him in 275 to return to Greece, where he achieved nothing decisive and was killed in a street fight in 272. By 270 Rome had taken all the Greek cities of Italy and was being further hellenized by its conquests. In 264 it moved on to Sicily, fought the Carthaginians there, and acquired most of the island in 241, though an adroit Greek ruler managed to keep Syracuse independent almost to the end of the century.

These events in the West were the ones decisive for the history of the world. If the Greeks of Sicily had been loyal to Pyrrhus an Epirote empire might have been created, strong enough to stop at least temporarily the advance of Rome. At the time, however, Macedon seemed much more important, not only to Pyrrhus but to all the world. The centers of civilization and luxury and (apparent) wealth and power were the capitals of the three kingdoms which had arisen from Alexander's empire. Beside these, the old Greek cities still enjoyed considerable prestige. Athens, in particular, was teacher of philosophy to the world. But it was recognized that as military powers they no longer mattered, and the latent power of the West was not yet realized. The history of the third century, there-

fore, as the Greeks of the third century saw it, was above
all the history of the three kingdoms.

Like the earlier history of Greece, it is a story of self-
destruction in futile border wars produced by the three
kingdoms' conflicting interests. The Antigonid kings of
Macedon inherited the Macedonian attempt to dominate
Greece. Also they had timber, tar, and agricultural products to sell to the Mediterranean cities and were therefore
concerned to keep the Aegean open to friendly traders.
The Seleucids inherited from the Persians and from Alexander a claim to control Asia Minor; they particularly
wanted the cities along its coast and along the Phoenician
coast, because these were the ports for the trade routes to
the east which ran across their territory. Finally, they also
inherited a claim to Palestine and if they had Palestine they
could hope to close off the northwestern end of some of
the competing trade routes across Arabia. The Ptolemies
of Egypt profited from those trade routes and were therefore determined to hold Palestine. Naval predominance
had given them the major ports of the Phoenician coast,
Cyprus and many Aegean islands, and coastal cities, from
which they got a considerable income. They hoped eventually to control the trade of the Aegean. Therefore they
were concerned to prevent both Macedonian domination
of the Greek cities and Seleucid control of Asia Minor.

From these conflicts of interest resulted the three "Syrian
Wars," fought off and on from 274 to 241. The principal
areas of fighting were northern Palestine, the Aegean, and
the coastal cities of Phoenicia and Asia Minor, but col-
lateral conflicts went on in mainland Greece and Cyrene.
In northern Palestine the Seleucid-Ptolemaic border was
pushed back and forth by raids and counterraids. The ter-

ritorial change was negligible; the most important consequence was a Ptolemaic program of city building and military settlement to strengthen Palestine. This greatly accelerated the hellenization of the country, with incalculable
consequences for the development of Judaism and, later, of
Christianity. Outside Palestine the principal instrument of
war was the Egyptian navy: besides direct sea battles it
was constantly active in seizing or defending places along
the coast, stirring up cities or local rulers to revolt from or
attack the Antigonids or Seleucids, and bringing help to
those who did so. The most important of its many protégés
turned out to be Eumenes I of Pergamum, who made his
city a center of power capable of standing against both
the Seleucids and the Galatians. The Antigonids and
Seleucids countered the Ptolemaic tactics by supporting
revolts against the Ptolemies in Cyrene and inciting Arab
attacks on the eastern border of the Delta.

The wars resulted in the discomfiture of all three kingdoms. A domestic upheaval in the Seleucid dynasty toward
the end of the 240's enabled Ptolemy III to march up the
Phoenician coast and inland perhaps as far as Mesopotamia
and to receive the nominal submission of the eastern territories. But he could not hold these conquests. The government of Egypt had become a bureaucracy so elaborate,
centralized, and insecure that it required his presence, and
so oppressive that the Greeks outside Egypt wanted none
of it. Ptolemy therefore returned to Egypt (with all the
loot he could carry). He left the Seleucid empire im-
poverished and divided by dynastic quarrels; for a long
time it could not threaten his Mediterranean possessions;
on this basis he made peace with it in 241. Just at that time,
however, the two Egyptian fleets in the Aegean were de-

stroyed by the Macedonians and their allies, the Rhodians. (The shift of Greek civilization to the East had made of Rhodes a shipping and banking center; as such it shared Macedon's concern to prevent Ptolemaic control of the Aegean.) Destruction of the Egyptian fleets made Macedonian domination of Greece a real possibility, but this possibility—and other circumstances—decided the Achaean and Aetolian leagues to co-operate in self-defense, and Macedon was presently worse off than before.

During the next twenty years (241–221) the three kingdoms were chiefly concerned with domestic problems. Ptolemy III neglected his army and navy for his magnificent court and for attempts to win over by patronage the native temples, which had long been centers of potential resistance to the government. Meanwhile his bureaucracy grew more cumbersome, as shown by the increasingly frequent records of misconduct of officers, peasants exhausted by the demands made on them and fleeing their lands, villages become desert because so many of the inhabitants have been imprisoned for nonpayment of taxes. By the time of the king's death in 221 the country was ready for revolt. Meanwhile the Seleucids were occupied by dynastic wars. This enabled their outlying territories to break away. Pergamum appropriated most of western and southern Asia Minor; the Galatians maintained themselves in the center; beyond the Caspian the Parthians overran Seleucid territory and cut off communications with the provinces farther to the east, which now became independent. Meanwhile in Macedonia the Antigonids had been harassed by attacks from barbarians to the north and would have been expelled from central and southern Greece had not the Greeks quarreled among themselves so bitterly that toward the end of the 220's the losers in the quarrel persuaded the Macedonians to come back and save them from their fellow Greeks.

By 221 it seemed that the kingdoms had passed their crises and were entering on a second period of power. A young and energetic ruler, Antiochus III, had come to the Seleucid throne in 223. In 221 Philip V of Macedon and Ptolemy IV of Egypt began their reigns. Antiochus set about reuniting the Seleucid territories. He tried to conquer Palestine, but was beaten off by Ptolemy IV. However, he later conquered Armenia and conducted a campaign to the east, as far as India, whence he brought back the nominal submissions of the former Seleucid territories and considerable booty. Philip V meanwhile confirmed his hold on Greece, defeated his enemies to the northwest, and then attempted to drive the Romans out of Illyria, where they had established themselves some years before to put down piracy and control the Adriatic. Rome was at this time in the throes of her second great war with Carthage; the Carthaginian general Hannibal had invaded Italy and was threatening the city. Philip reached an agreement with Hannibal. Rome allied with Philip's enemies in Greece and also with Pergamum, which saw itself threatened by the increase of Macedonian power in the Aegean. So long as Rome was busy with Carthage, Philip held his own, but he was persuaded to make a separate peace in 205 and Carthage was forced to surrender in 201. This left Rome free to deal with Philip, and an occasion was at hand.

The attack of Antiochus III on Egypt, fifteen years before, had forced Ptolemy IV to train and arm native Egyptians to supplement his Greek forces. Thereafter

Egyptian resentment of the Greeks and lower-class resentment of the government had expressed themselves in revolts which tore the country to pieces. Ptolemy had died in 205, leaving a child heir to the throne, and Philip and Antiochus thereupon had agreed to partition the Egyptian territories. Antiochus now (202–198) seized Palestine, while Philip attacked the Egyptian possessions around the Hellespont. This frightened Rhodes, Pergamum, and Athens. They appealed to Rome and Rome was happy to defend them. Philip was defeated in 197 and confined to Macedonia. Antiochus took this opportunity to subjugate much of Asia Minor and advance into Thrace. This again frightened Pergamum, which again appealed to Rome. Meanwhile the Roman policy of supporting oligarchies, and Roman arrogance and severity, had alienated many Greeks, while others had been angered at failing to get what they wanted in the settlement with Philip. The Greek tradition of looking for some ally against a powerful ally now led many Greeks to appeal to Antiochus. The resultant war practically ended with the defeat of Antiochus at Magnesia in 190. Thereafter no power nor combination of powers in the Mediterranean basin could stand against Rome with any hope of success. The Greek cities and kingdoms alike had effectively become subjects of the Roman republic. More than a century and a half of extortion, rebellion, resubjugation, renewed extortion, renewed rebellion and so on, were to intervene before the last of the great hellenistic kingdoms, Egypt, was appropriated by Augustus in 30 B.C. But all that belongs to the history of Rome. In 190 the Greek states became elements of the Roman world.

The year 190 B.C. was almost a hundred and fifty years after the Macedonian conquest of Greece in 338. During those hundred and fifty years Greek civilization had been transformed from the culture of a network of cities and small states bordering the Mediterranean, to the culture of the ruling classes controlling not only the Mediterranean basin but also southwestern Asia as far as the Indus valley and the approches of Tibet. The Parthians rapidly appropriated Greek achievements; the Greeks in the eastern provinces of the Seleucid empire retained control there until the latter half of the second century B.C., then reconquered northwestern India and ruled there for another century. It is true that even in these newly conquered countries the culture did not remain exclusively upper class, and in Greece itself and in the old Greek colonies the lower classes remained predominantly Greek, although with a large admixture of slaves and resident aliens. But it is typical of the hellenistic age, as this period is called, that even when the lower class remains Greek, its importance to the culture declines. In politics, the world is dominated by the kings and their generals; in war, the citizen army and navy are hopelessly outclassed by professionals; professional actors, singers, dancers and athletes dominate the festivals; in all fields of endeavor it is the upper class which sets the style and the professional who turns out the product; the poor, whether Greek, Italian or Syrian, follow along as best they can.

This transformation of Greek culture from a civic phenomenon to an international upper-class characteristic was not effected everywhere at the same time nor in the same fashion.

In Greece matters moved slowly. Alexander's establishment of Greeks as a ruling class in Egypt and southwestern Asia had created a vast and wealthy market for the skills and wares of Greece. The Greeks abroad were not at first satisfied with local imitations of products they had known; they wanted the real things and were able to pay for them. So they were followed by Greek merchants, artisans, artists, entertainers, and professional men, who further swelled the market for native Greek products. Conquest and business drained from Greece the homeless men who had burdened the cities and helped produce wars and revolutions. So long as Alexander lived peace was maintained, the routes were open for trade and trade was encouraged by Alexander's abundant and uniform currency. All these causes produced in Greece, particularly at Athens, a period of prosperity which lasted into the beginning of the third century. This brief prosperity, saw the final flowering of Athenian culture—new pottery types appeared; sculpture turned to new fields, especially portraits of philosophers and literary men, with notable success; in nearby Tanagra the manufacture of terra-cotta statuettes was raised to a fine art; the "new comedy" turned from burlesque and politics to the intrigues of private life in well-to-do families and created the pattern to be followed by comedies throughout western literature; philosophy developed new creeds which could appeal especially to the well-to-do layman. By 275, however, not only Athens, but all Greece, had entered on a long decline. The men, the money, and the military power had gone elsewhere; the trade was about to follow them. Prosperity was undermined by the chronic local wars and the long struggle against the Macedonians. Cultural importance declined along with prosperity. Philosophy, as represented by endowed institutions, continued at Athens, but the arts and the sciences went with the trade to the capitals of the hellenistic kingdoms.

The kingdoms differed greatly.

Macedonia was a feudal monarchy with a wild northern frontier and an aristocracy more concerned about boar-hunting than belles-lettres. Its wealth came from its gold and silver mines, forests (material for shipbuilding), and fields. A few big cities were scattered along the coast. The kings patronized a circle of artists and scholars. But except as a political and military force the country was the least significant of the three major kingdoms.

The Seleucid kingdom was a chaos of territories of different types—Greek cities new and old, Near Eastern cities more or less remodeled on Greek lines, states controlled by oriental temples or hereditary nobles, or granted by the kings to their ministers or favorites, tribal territories, and so on. The task of the Seleucid rulers was to hold this chaos together. To unite their subjects to themselves they followed Alexander's example and had themselves deified. But for practical purposes they relied on three things: territorial governors with military support, the royal standing army, and the network of Greek cities which they had inherited from Alexander and had themselves greatly increased by founding new cities along the trade routes which crossed their kingdom and were, after agriculture, the principal source of its wealth. These Greek cities depended for protection from the surrounding barbarians first on themselves, then on the territorial governors and their forces, and in the last resort on the royal army. Therefore they were expected to be centers of royalist influence in their districts and to serve as bases for military operations in case of need. Some of them prospered, survived the fall of the Seleucids, and remained centers of Greek culture in the Parthian empire for another five hundred years. In them, but even more in the old, Near Eastern cities where the Greeks settled, went on the mutual modification of Greek and Near Eastern cultural traditions. This was to have important consequences in Roman times, especially in the field of religion. Meanwhile the Greek cities of the kingdom and the royal court provided an important market for writers, philosophers, and artists from Greece, and sent back to Greece a number of students who distinguished themselves in the philosophical schools.

Ptolemaic Egypt was a masterpiece of royal absolutism. Apart from the capital, Alexandria, and the southern capital, Ptolemaïs, there was no Greek city of importance. The native towns were governed as part of the country-side. The Greeks and Macedonians were settled in villages as farmers and were directly governed by royal officials. The King was worshiped as a god by the Greeks; so, often, was his consort. As Pharaoh he was worshiped as a god by the Egyptians, and the immense Egyptian temples, with their teeming priesthoods and vast landholdings, were directly subject to him. For Greeks and Eygptians alike the government was the King's household and the country his estate. All aspects of economic life were regulated by his steward. What land was to be planted, what it was to be planted with, where and for how much the crops were to be sold, transportation, processing and manufacture, wholesale and retail trade, import and export, banking—nothing escaped supervision and taxation, and many trades were royal monopolies. The system required an immense bureaucracy which became ruinously expensive and oppressive, with political consequences already described.

The center of the system, where all the wealth it could squeeze from the country was concentrated, was the royal court in Alexandria. Here hellenistic culture reached its acme. Not only were the Ptolemies lavish patrons of the arts, but they turned their genius for organization to the patronage of science and scholarship. A royal institute was founded on the model of the Platonic academy, as an association for the worship of the Muses, whence its name, the Museum; royal funds provided for the support of teachers and for gardens, dining halls, lecture halls, and the collection of an immense library. Throughout most of the third century, therefore, Alexandria was the center of artistic and intellectual life in every field except philosophy, where Athens remained pre-eminent. But this brilliance was paid for by the denial of Greek city life to the rest of the country, with the consequence that the civic tradition of Greece was never communicated to the natives of Egypt as it was to those of Syria. At most the Greek alphabet was gradually modified to replace the old Egyptian script. Greek plastic and graphic arts eventually altered the native tradition somewhat more than it did them, and something of Greek philosophic and religious thought eventually penetrated, chiefly in the form of Christianity.

Besides the major kingdoms, further variations of the hellenistic pattern were provided by the minor states.

The rulers of Pergamum imitated their allies, the Ptolemies, and built up a centralized monarchy with a brilliant court supported by a suppressed countryside. They too were patrons of learning and of the arts. In sculpture the Pergamene school did the most heroic and dramatic work which the hellenistic period produced—a great frieze of gods battling giants, to commemorate the defeat of the savage Galatians. In practical matters the city was no less eminent. The technique developed for the preparation of the leather on which the books of its great library were written has given us the word "parchment" (*pergamena*), and material so prepared was what preserved through the middle ages almost all such ancient literature as did survive.

By contrast to Pergamum, Rhodes carried on the tradition of the Greek city-state, maintained a moderate democracy and an efficient fleet supported by overseas trade, beat off the Antigonids with help from the Ptolemies and the Ptolemies with help from the Antigonids, erected its famous colossus, and was the residence of a number of artists, writers, and philosophers. In Syracuse the traditions of Greek tyranny were revived, but besides tyrants the city produced a number of eminent scientists. Even more diverse, and more important, was the hellenization of the ruling classes of Rome and Parthia, which lies outside the limits of this account.

Through all these different hellenistic states runs the uniformity of hellenistic culture. Already in the age of colonization men from various parts of Greece had begun to feel they were all Greeks together, by contrast with Italians or Egyptians or Persians. The feeling grew stronger now they found themselves in the middle of Egypt or Persia; the common elements of their Greek tradition were preserved, the local peculiarities disappeared. At the same time, closer acquaintance with the natives of the country they now ruled made them more clearly aware of the similarity of all men. Not only personal ties, but also the mere awareness of common humanity bound together, on occasion, most diverse elements of the population of the hellenistic kingdoms. This began to break down the ethnic limits of the Greek community. The philosophers of the age developed the doctrine of the brotherhood of man; the term

"Greek" came to be used of anyone who possessed the common culture.

One of the more convenient manifestations of the new community of culture was the gradual introduction of common points of reference for dating. Hitherto documents had been dated by reference to the chief officer of the state in which they were written; if he held office for several years in succession the reference was made precise by specification of the year. Thus Athenian documents were dated by specifying that so-and-so was Archon; Persian, by giving the name of the Great King and the year of his reign ("Year three of Artaxerxes, the King," or the like). Given the multiplicity of tiny states and the frequent change of officers, the result was chaos. Under the Seleucids it became common to date events from the year when the dynasty came to power (312), while in Alexandria it became a practice of scholars to date events from the first Olympic games of which the victors were recorded (supposedly those of 776). Both methods achieved wide success, were perpetuated for centuries, and served as models for the Christian and Jewish practices of reckoning from the supposed years of Jesus' birth and of the creation of the world.

Among the most important of the local peculiarities which now disappear outside Greece are those of speech. Ancient Greek had been spoken in many dialects, and each dialect had been rich in special words and forms. Now Greeks from all parts of the world were thrown together and had to make themselves understood to each other and to the natives they ruled, while the natives had to learn Greek and often learned no more than they had to. The simplified Greek of native servants became the native tongue of the Greek children they cared for. Classical Greek became a learned language, preserved and imitated in great and would-be-great literature. Between it and the language of the street ranged the everyday speech of cultivated men, with its subspecies, the jargons of the various professions. This was the language of the cities and the courts, which were the centers of hellenistic culture, and it was not the least achievement of that culture to produce this simplified, international language, which facilitated communication throughout the whole civilized world.

As the language was partially a learned language, so the whole culture was, to an extent, something learned, not to say, affected. In Rome and Parthia this was obvious, but it was also true in the native kingdoms of Asia Minor and in the Macedonian courts of Egypt, the Seleucid kingdom, and Macedon itself. Even in Greece there was a deliberate adjustment to the new facts of the outside world, to the new Greek culture which was no longer the native culture of Greece: the Athenians learned to worship the international hellenistic deities sponsored by Pergamum and Alexandria; their children were taught to use the new engines of war developed by the engineers of the hellenistic kings; in their philosophic schools philosophers from the Near East taught them in a language still Greek, but hardly Attic.

The extent of the difference between this new culture and the culture of classical Greece—Greece of the fifth century—can be indicated by six contrasts: (1) In the classical world the principal form of land tenure was the relatively small holding of the ordinary citizen; in the hellenistic world it was the large estate of the king, the temple or the great official. (2) In the classical world the chief political form was the city-state, of small extent and homogeneous population, with some form of conciliar government; in the hellenistic world—though the appearance of local autonomy was often preserved, and the fact occasionally survived—the chief political form was the absolute monarchy ruling various peoples and a vast territory. (3) In the classical world the structure of society was regulated chiefly by local custom and tradition; in the hellenistic world a much larger part than before was played by explicit, written laws enforced by alien rulers throughout wide domains. (4) In the classical world the traditional cult of the gods of the city was the center both of petition and of patriotism; in the hellenistic world patriotism found expression in the cult of the divine ruler, while petitions were more often directed to deities whose political affiliations, if any, were of minor importance. (5) In the classical world, because the economic and political units were so small, private individuals were of relatively great importance; this both encouraged their concern for the state and made their activities matters of public concern; consequently the artistic and philosophical life of the period was closely connected with politics and politics was a major concern of the average man. In the hellenistic world, because the units were so big, private persons were generally of no importance; accordingly they neglected the state and the state them; therefore the artistic and philosophical life of this period was generally nonpolitical (except when inspired by patronage or the hope of patronage), and the average man was less interested in politics, more in his private affairs. (6) In the classical world the civil administration and the army were largely run by amateurs (civilians ordinarily employed in private occupations); professionals were rarely used except as subordinates; therefore the internal histories of the states were full of struggles between political factions. In the hellenistic world both the administration and the army were usually staffed by professionals and the internal history was therefore one of bureaucratic intrigues and palace revolutions.

Most of these contrasts resulted from developments which had already begun in the earlier years of the fourth century, when classical culture was disintegrating. This was particularly true of military professionalism. But in the hellenistic world the growth of professionalism and the consequences of the professional approach were obvious everywhere: increased technical proficiency, collection of previous knowledge, systemization and consequent discoveries, mostly minor; reduction of the system to a handbook and a set of rules, making basic discoveries more difficult; consequent standardization of products, with gain in average quality and loss of individuality.

The development of professionalism is part of a general turning of Greek thought toward practical questions, which resulted from the administrative necessities and opportunities confronting the Greeks as rulers of large countries. Governments wanted professionals who could assure them of specific results. For such men careers were open. The city building of the Seleucids, the economic organization of the Ptolemies, the agricultural and military programs of all the great powers, made possible undertakings and rewards on a scale undreamt of by the city-states. War, for example, was completely transformed by the increased use of cavalry, bowmen, and slingers, the introduction of elephants, the development of siege engines, and the great increase in the size of armies. Forces involved in single conflicts numbered up to about 75,000 on a side, and the total military force of the Seleucids must have been about double this. Besides the increase in scale, the fact that the kings were absolute rulers enabled their ministers to carry through projects which the elected officials of a city-state would never have dared suggest, for example the development of the techniques of economic control in Ptolemaic Egypt.

With the extension of resources and power went an extension of knowledge which made possible the conception of new projects. Alexander not only conquered the Persian empire, but explored it. He took with him a staff of engineers, architects, and geographers and collected data on the plants and animals of the countries along his route. At the same time explorers pushed beyond the other frontiers of Greek settlement. In particular Pytheas of Massilia, a few years after Alexander's death, circumnavigated Britain, discovered the Scandinavian peninsula and may have sighted Iceland. The information so gathered was codified and extended by later scholarship and put to practical use by the kings, especially the Ptolemies, who were concerned to introduce valuable plants and animals to their realms. Greek astronomy learned much from Babylonia, and Greek medicine something from Egypt. Royal patronage made possible further research in all fields and the results of research were at the service of the kings. The centralization of government was accompanied by a centralization of knowledge, and the growth of bureaucracy by a growth of information about the country governed, a detailed knowledge of the society and how it worked, which encouraged further attempts to manage it. (In Egypt, the Ptolemaic secret police were everywhere.)

This accumulation of knowledge necessitated attempts to systematize it, including scientific speculation. In mathematics (Euclid), physics (Archimedes), mathematical geography (Eratosthenes), and botany (Theophrastus), the theories, discoveries, and formulations of this age remained standard for the ancient world and became, either directly or through later reworkings, the points of departure for the Renaissance. In astronomy, Aristarchus at this time argued that the earth went round the sun, but he was refuted in the second century by Hipparchus.

Along with these scientific achievements came the application of scientific method to the study of the humanities: the collection, classification, and edition of texts, the production of histories of literature and philosophy, of critical theories based on literary history, and of poems written according to critical theories are all achievements of the hellenistic age and especially of the scholars in the libraries of Alexandria and Pergamum. Their editorial work shaped the intellectual history of the western world, for the works preserved and explained by their editing became "the classics," the texts regularly used in education.

Given the recognition of a body of classics, the authors of the hellenistic age had to choose between deliberate imitation and deliberate originality. "Classicism" as an artistic manner now became possible. But even works in the classical manner must justify themselves by some novelty. The important literary achievement of the age was a new type of literature, belles-lettres, the polite literature of everyday life, which pleases by wit, verbal facility, some small originality or touch of sentiment, or the brief creation of an imaginary world, such as the country life for city people which is conjured into being by the idyls of Theocritus, a world of bucolic fantasy where the hardship and coarseness of the real countryside are forgotten. The short poem and shorter epigram were the most successful forms of this literature of amusement and of something more, which concentrated in couplets the passion and pathos of men who knew themselves not to be heroes.

Thus in every field, thought and expression was shaped by awareness of the extent of history, the breadth of the world. It was the accumulation of knowledge that produced professionalism, directed governmental policy, stimulated the sciences, and weighed down the literature.

But the larger the world and the state became, the more alone men found themselves. The city-state had been home; the Seleucid or Ptolemaic kingdom was merely where you lived. The kings attempted to provide symbols for loyalty by self-deification and the establishment of royal cults, but the effort had little success. Many Greeks turned to the worship of Near Eastern deities, but this usually had nothing to do with the question of loyalty: you did not usually go to a god to love him, nor to be loved; you went for a specific favor—a cure for some ailment, for instance —but if the god happened to grant it this did not necessarily make him an object of your wholehearted devotion. You paid him what you had promised, you recommended him to your friends, but you did not henceforth live for him the way your great-great-great-grandfather had lived for Athens. You lived for yourself.

This individualism appeared everywhere in the history of the age. The political history bristled with individuals, not to say egomaniacs. The deification of rulers showed the importance attributed, at least officially, to the individuals deified. In the plastic arts, portraiture was the form most characteristic of the age. Both the plastic arts and literature appealed constantly to the private patron and his (or, very often, her) taste for the sentimental, the pretty and the cute. Even grotesque objects are of interest for themselves; the schematized grotesques of classical times are supplemented by accurate studies of old age, drunkenness, and disease. The isolation of individuals and their attempt to overcome it appears in a great increase in the number of clubs and other voluntary organizations, especially religious ones.

But it was in philosophy that individualism found its fullest expression, notably in the teachings of Epicurus and of the Stoics, beginning with Zeno, from whose practice of teaching in a public portico, *stoa*, the school derived its name.

Epicurus began by accepting Aristippus' observations: the goal of life is happiness and happiness is derived from pleasure. This lead him to analyze pleasure and conclude that its most important form is mere, contented, undisturbed existence. That there were more vivid pleasures he did not deny, but he observed that they often were more trouble to get, or to have had, than they were worth. The wise man will do his best to live an untroubled life, he will withdraw from public affairs to his house and his garden, limit his desires, and live, by careful economy, on his investments. (He is evidently a middle-class Athenian citizen in the period of prosperity following Alexander's conquests). For pleasure and protection he will surround himself with a circle of friends, but will avoid love as a disturbance. For security's sake he will obey the laws and get on well with his neighbors. Thus with good luck and good management he will be secure against everything but disease. Disease is usually bearable. If unbearable it can be stopped by suicide. Death is not an evil, but merely the cessation of individual existence, the dissipation of that arrangement of atoms which constitutes the soul. Therefore there is nothing to fear in death or after it. The common stories about the gods and a life after death are nonsense. It is not to be denied that the gods exist and are perfect, but because they are perfect they must be perfectly happy and to be perfectly happy they must be utterly indifferent to human affairs. They are to be worshiped as ideals.

These opinions were bolstered by a physics (which explained the world as the result of chance combinations of atoms), a consequent theory of knowledge, and other requisites for a system of philosophy, but the main concern was the way of life. In Epicurus' own garden was formed a new philosophic school, and the property was handed down from generation to generation of his followers. He was honored as a god who had revealed to men the way of salvation; his writings were preserved as sacred scripture. Their influence spread far beyond the limits of his school and shaped much of the thought and more of the life of the hellenistic and Roman worlds.

Zeno and the Stoics followed the line taken by Antisthenes and Diogenes, but with decent moderation. They accepted the notion that the goal of life is happiness and defined happiness as life according to virtue, or nature, or reason. To the ordinary Greek it might have seemed unlikely that acting virtuously, acting naturally, and acting reasonably should be identical, but the Stoics, like the Epicureans, defended their theory by a made-to-order physics: nature is essentially a rational fire which acts upon itself to make of itself the more stable elements and thus the world. The order of the world is the expression of this reason (*logos*) which at once constitutes and creates and permeates and governs the world. To act in accordance with this directive reason, inherent in nature, is virtue. The argument is stronger than it seems at first sight, since reason is presumably a reflection of the apparent order of nature (as well as vice versa) and men's notions of virtue and happiness are unquestionably shaped by both nature and reason. But these approximations are so loose that the argument built on them cannot account for the strength of Stoicism, which became the leading missionary philosophy of antiquity, eventually converted a ruler of the Roman empire and was one of the major factors which gradually changed the temper of the ancient world.

The strength of Stoicism came from two things: the way of life practiced and the security offered. The way of life was the way of asceticism, of self-examination, self-control, daily training in neglect of the passions, and attention to the dictates of conscience. The security was contentment in the consciousness of virtue. This enabled the Stoic to participate in the world and yet be indifferent to it. Many teachers of the school held that a man was duty bound to take part in the political life of his state. But the wise man would do this as a duty. Therefore, whether his political efforts succeeded or failed, he would remain content in the consciousness that he had done his duty, the blissful awareness of his own virtue. The Stoics represented this as sufficient for happiness and undertook by training to make it so. For the man happy in his own virtue is free. He cannot be bribed, for he has all he wants. He cannot be threatened, for nothing can take from him the only thing about which he is concerned. He can be killed, but death is not an evil: that virtue which was embodied in him will persist in the order of the world and must ultimately triumph. By this confidence he knows himself truly a citizen, not of a city or kingdom, but of the world; he finds all men his brothers; he is at one with nature and with himself.

The differences of Stoicism and Epicureanism, especially of the systems of physics with which they were buttressed, made them bitter enemies. But beneath the differences of terminology, the two systems were surprisingly similar. Both were ultimately concerned with the individual, not the city nor the state. Both took for granted that the individual's goal in life should be happiness, and both equated happiness with tranquillity (for Epicurus, undisturbedness, for the Stoics, self-sufficiency). Both thought a man could attain happiness by his own efforts, in particular, by the use of reason and the practice of self-discipline—ascetic limitation of desires, and thus of fears and griefs, and deliberate concentration on the pleasure to be derived from self-satisfaction. Both were individual adjustments to the insecurity and indifference of the hellenistic world. What could be done? One could withdraw from the world, practice frugality, live content in the enjoyment of one's wisdom, and face death without fear. Or one could by practice achieve indifference to misfortune, follow unhesitatingly the moral teaching of the sect, live content in the enjoyment of one's virtue, and face death with assurance.

Chronological Summary

c. 560–510 Pisistratid tyranny in Athens.

c.   547 Persian conquest of Lydia.

c. 525–475 Flowering of southern Italy and Sicily: Pythagoras, Xenophanes, Parmenides.

c. 500–325 Attic red-figure pottery.

    500 Revolt of Ionian cities from Persians.

492–479 Persian attempt to conquer Greece; Carthaginian attack on Sicily (battles of Marathon, 490; Thermopylae, Salamis, and Himera, 480; Plataea and Mycale, 479).

    478 Organization of Delian League (beginning of Athenian empire).
          Aeschylus, Pindar.

461–430 Pericles in power. Sophocles, Euripides, Herodotus, Hippodamus of Miletus, the sophists, Phidias.

431–404 Peloponnesian War. Aristophanes, Thucydides, Socrates, Hippocrates.

406–367 Tyranny of Dionysius I in Syracuse.

404–371 Spartan pre-eminence in Greece (chief wars, 400–386 and 379–371). Antisthenes, Aristippus, Xenophon.

    399 Condemnation and execution of Socrates.

    393 Rebuilding of long walls of Athens.

371–362 Theban pre-eminence, Epaminondas.
          Plato.

359–336 Reign of Philip II of Macedon.
          Demosthenes, Isocrates, Diogenes, Aristotle, Praxiteles.

357–355 Revolt of Athens' eastern Aegean allies, instigated by Mausolus of Caria.

357–340 Civil war in Sicily.

    338 Battle of Chaironea. Philip II in control of Greece.

336–323 Reign of Alexander the Great.
323–276 Wars for control of the parts of Alexander's empire. Emergence of Ptolemaic, Seleucid, and Antigonid kingdoms, Bithynia and Pontus.
Last flowering of Athenian culture: portrait statues, Tanagra terracottas, new comedy, Theophrastus, Epicurus, Zeno.
317–289 Agathocles tyrant of Syracuse.
280–275 Campaigns of Pyrrhus in Italy and Sicily.
279–278 Galatians overrun Macedonia, northern Greece, and Thrace and cross into Asia Minor.
274–241 Syrian Wars I–III.
Alexandria center of civilization.
270 Rome in control of all Greek cities of Italy.
241 End of Rome's first war with Carthage. Rome acquires most of Sicily.
241–221 Decay of Egypt, defeats of Macedon, dynastic wars in Seleucid kingdom. Pergamum and Parthia increase in power.
221–190 Attempted restoration of Macedonian power by Philip V; of Seleucid, by Antiochus III.
203 Philip and Antiochus agree to partition outlying territories of Ptolemy V.
201 End of Rome's second war with Carthage. Rome supreme in western Mediterranean.
197 Philip V defeated by Rome.
190 Battle of Magnesia. Antiochus III defeated by Rome.

Suggestions for Further Reading

THE most important things in Greek history were the things the Greeks thought, said, wrote, carved, modeled, and painted. Most of the major works of Greek literature are readily available in numerous translations (and it is worth while to read a work in several translations, to see several of the different meanings which different translators have given it). For the physical remains, J. Boardman, *Greek Art* (New York, 1964), is a first-rate survey, and R. Lullies and M. Hirmer, *Greek Sculpture* (New York, 1957), contains superb photographs; M. Bieber, *The Sculpture of the Hellenistic Age* (New York, 1955), is the best historical study of the later work and is also well illustrated, as is A. Lawrence, *Greek Architecture* (Harmondsworth, 1957). E. Pfuhl, *Masterpieces of Greek Drawing and Painting* (tr. by J. Beazley, 2d ed.; London, 1955), is a classic; R. Cook, *Greek Painted Pottery* (London, 1960), bids fair to become one; and C. Seltman, *Greek Coins* (2d ed.; London, 1955), affords a good introduction to those works of Greek art which have done most to illustrate political history. Political and social history have been further illustrated by inscriptions, of which a selection will be found translated in G. Botsford and E. Sihler, *Hellenic Civilization* (New York, 1915), and papyri, of which many are translated in A. Hunt and C. Edgar, *Select Papyri*, Vol. I, "Private Affairs"; Vol. II, "Public Documents" (Loeb Library, 1952 and 1956).

Of historical works, J. Bury, *A History of Greece to the Death of Alexander the Great* (3d ed., rev. by R. Meiggs; London, 1956), and N. Hammond, *A History of Greece to 322 B.C.* (Oxford, 1959), give good single-volume surveys of their subject. A fuller treatment of the fifth and fourth centuries will be found in M. Laistner, *The Greek World from 479 to 323* (3d ed.; London, 1957). W. Tarn, *Hellenistic Civilisation* (3d ed., rev. by G. Griffith, London, 1952), is the best handbook for the later period, but see also M. Cary, *A History of the Greek World from 323–146 B.C.* (2d ed.; London, 1951). For questions of detail consult *The Oxford Classical Dictionary* (Oxford, 1949); for fuller discussion and listing of sources, see *The Cambridge Ancient History*, Vols. I–VII (Cambridge, 1924–1928), though the earlier volumes, especially, need correction and many chapters of the new edition of Vols. I and II are already in print separately.

Of the many readable works in English on aspects of Greek history and civilization, the following are noteworthy: A. Andrews, *The Greek Tyrants* (London, 1956); J. Boardman, *The Greeks Overseas* (Harmondsworth, 1964); J. Bury, *The Ancient Greek Historians* (London, 1909, reprinted 1958); M. Cary and E. Warmington, *The Ancient Explorers* (London, 1929); E. Dodds, *The Greeks and the Irrational* (reprint; Boston, 1957); D. Dudley, *A History of Cynicism* (London, 1937); T. Dunbabin, *The Western Greeks* (Oxford, 1948); V. Ehrenberg, *The Greek State* (Oxford, 1960); W. Ferguson, *Hellenistic Athens* (London, 1911); A. Festugière, *Epicurus and His Gods* (tr. by C. Chilton; Oxford, 1955); R. Flickinger, *The Greek Theater and Its Drama* (Chicago, 1960); M. Hadas, *Hellenistic Culture* (New York, 1959); W. Jaeger, *Aristotle* (tr. by R. Robinson, 2d ed.; Oxford, 1948), *Paideia, the Ideals of Greek Culture* (tr. by G. Highet, 3 vols.; New York, 1943–1945), and *The Theology of the Early Greek Philosophers* (Oxford, 1947); H. Marrou, *A History of Education in An-*

tiquity (tr. by G. Lamb; New York, 1956); G. Murray, *Five Stages of Greek Religion* (London, 1935) and *The Rise of the Greek Epic* (4th ed.; Oxford, 1934); M. Nilsson, *Greek Piety* (tr. by H. Rose; Oxford, 1948), *A History of Greek Religion* (2d ed.; tr. by F. Fielden; Oxford, 1949), and *Homer and Mycenae* (London, 1933); A. Nock, *Conversion* (Oxford, 1933); E. Rohde, *Psyche, the Cult of Souls and Belief in Immortality among the Greeks* (tr. by W. Hillis; London, 1925); W. Ross, *Aristotle* (5th ed.; London, 1956); M. Rostovtzeff, *The Social and Economic History of the Hellenistic World* (3 vols.; Oxford, 1941); S. Sambursky, *The Physical World of the Greeks* (tr. by M. Dagut; London, 1956) and *Physics of the Stoics* (London, 1959); E. Schrödinger, *Nature and the Greeks* (Cambridge, Eng., 1954); P. Shorey, *What Plato Said* (Chicago, 1933, reprinted 1958); W. Tarn, *Alexander the Great* (2 vols.; Cambridge, Eng., 1948), *Antigonos Gonatas* (Oxford, 1913), and *The Greeks in Bactria and India* (2d ed.; Cambridge, Eng., 1951); V. Tcherikover, *Hellenistic Civilization and the Jews* (tr. by S. Applebaum; Philadelphia, 1959); J. Thompson, *History of Ancient Geography* (Cambridge, Eng., 1948); R. Wycherley, *How the Greeks Built Cities* (2d ed., London, 1962); A. Zimmern, *The Greek Commonwealth* (5th ed.; Oxford, 1931).

Index